WHAT PEOPLE ARE SAYING ABOUT

ESCAPING GAZA

"Sad and shocking. I never kn
Caitlin White (17 years old)

"The scale of this tragedy will haunt the world."
Michelle White (Counsellor)

"This true story reveals the cruelty of war!"
Louisa Harding (Mental Health Nurse)

"Sad, strong, honest."
Steven Rees (Mental Health Nurse)

"Helps us to understand the damage of war."
Conan Thomas Hammett (Army Officer)

"Enlightening. Helps people to understand what a refugee goes through."
Lianne Lynch (Red Cross Worker)

"A riveting read. You feel as if it is your own story."
Mitchell Chadwick (Hotel Industry Worker)

"Compelling reading about the horrific journey of a refugee."
Diane Spick (Gas Connection Specialist)

"Sadness and tragedy interspersed with hope. The resilient human spirit shines through."
Denise Zammitt (Psychologist)

Escaping Gaza

Raed Zanoon the Peace Seeker

Escaping Gaza

Raed Zanoon the Peace Seeker

Dr Julie-Anne Sykley

&

Raed Zanoon

BOOKS

Winchester, UK
Washington, USA

First published by O-Books, 2016
O-Books is an imprint of John Hunt Publishing Ltd., Laurel House, Station Approach,
Alresford, Hants, SO24 9JH, UK
office1@jhpbooks.net
www.johnhuntpublishing.com

For distributor details and how to order please visit the 'Ordering' section on our website.

Text copyright: Julie-Anne Sykley and Raed Zanoon 2015

ISBN: 978 1 78535 221 8
Library of Congress Control Number: 2015955998

All rights reserved. Except for brief quotations in critical articles or reviews, no part of this
book may be reproduced in any manner without prior written permission from the publishers.

The rights of Julie-Anne Sykley and Raed Zanoon as authors have been asserted in accordance
with the Copyright, Designs and Patents Act 1988.

A CIP catalogue record for this book is available from the British Library.

Design: Stuart Davies

Printed in the USA by Edwards Brothers Malloy

We operate a distinctive and ethical publishing philosophy in all
areas of our business, from our global network of authors to
production and worldwide distribution.

CONTENTS

Welcome   1

1. Trapped   5
2. Arabian Nights   10
3. Rafah Backstreets (2003)   18
4. Muslim Bride (2004)   29
5. Targeted (2006)   38
6. Gaza Burning (2007–2009)   49
7. Palestine "Peace Dove"   56
8. Gridlocked   65
9. Dark Jakartan Jungles (2013)   77
10. Outback Days   86

References   106

Raed Zanoon

Raed, who speaks Arabic, is from the Gaza Strip of Palestine where he lived for 29 years. In 2013, he came to Australia as a refugee. Now Raed lives in Darwin in the Northern Territory where he works as a Red Cross volunteer, attends the Darwin Baptist Church, is learning to drive a car, and is fast becoming a well-known character in the community. Due to his lifelong exposure to war and being shot by an terrorist, Raed still experiences medical problems, physical disability, and depression and nightmares so bad that sometimes he must stay in hospital. Raed would like to open a kebab shop one day and cook Middle Eastern food for people. A devoted father and son, Raed is very keen to give his family a better life and his dream is to reunite with them one day. Raed wants people to know that most refugees who come to Australia are "not terrorists; they are trying to get away from them." No matter how traumatic life has been, Raed says, "it is important to get on with everyone" in the world.

Dr Julie-Anne Sykley

Dr Julie-Anne Sykley loves adventure (both outdoors and inside the imagination). Julie-Anne is also an Australian Psychologist with more than 25 years professional experience helping people to deal with a wide range of mental health issues. From inner city Sydney to the remote Territory outback, she has assisted young people, adults, offenders, prisoners, traditional Aboriginal people, and refugees from the Middle East, Asia and other places. Julie-Anne wants to increase people's power to overcome hardship, which is why she co-wrote this book for you. Julie-Anne currently assists people with depression, anxiety, post-traumatic stress, suicidal thinking, and other mental health issues in the Northern Territory where she lives with lightning, cyclones, and crocodiles.

Raed's Acknowledgements

Thank you Australian Navy – you saved everyone on the boat and gave us food and water. Without you, I would not be here to write this today.

Thank you Australian Immigration Department – you gave me a chance to live in peace and you help many refugees.

Thank you IHMS (International Health and Medical Services) – you were very kind and caring.

Thanks Serco – for watching over me when I was sick and for playing games with me like snooker and cards. You made me feel safe for the first time in my life.

To the Australian Red Cross – thank you Sarah Kavanagh (Manager), Constanze ("Tani") de Greenlaw (Store Manager), Lianne Lynch, and many others.

To the Darwin Baptist Church and Pastor Warren Douglas – thank you for sharing Christian messages about hope, love and peace.

Many Thanks also to:

Seyed Hossein Mousavi (Marine Engineer, Iran/Australia)

Ameer Younan (Assyrian/Arabic Interpreter, Australia)

Gail Davison (Mental Health Nurse, Australia)

Tania Ferguson (Australia)

Julie Zanoon (Gaza/United Kingdom) – for all your checking, editing and research.

Raed's Family

Raed's Parents

Abdul Hakim Zanoon (Father, 1961–) + Alia (Mother, 1961–)

13 Children altogether. In birth order, these are:

1. Izdhar (sister, 1981–1986)

2. Amira (sister, 1983–)

3. Raed (self, 1984–)

4. Izdhar2 (sister, 1986–)

5. Ayman (brother, 1987–)

6. Achraf (brother, 1988–)

7. Anhar (sister, 1990–)

8. Amjad (brother, 1992–)

9. Adham (brother, 1994–)

10. Inas (sister, 1996–)

11. Abdulla (brother, 1999–)

12. Saddam (brother, 2002–)

13. Nada (sister, 2009–)

Raed's Timeline

My country of birth: Palestine
My language: Arabic
My official nationality: Stateless
I lived in Gaza almost my whole life.
At the age of 29 years, I left Gaza forever.

Age (years):
0 – Born 27th May 1984 in Rafah Refugee Camp (inside the Gaza Strip).
1 –
2 –
3 –
4 –
5 –
6 – Attended Rafah Preparatory School, inside the refugee camp (6 years).
7 –
8 –
9 –
10 –
11 –
12 – Worked in a metal factory (6 years).
13 –
14 –
15 –
16 –
17 –
18 –
19 – Married Asma. Started working in a clothes store (2004).
20 –
21 – Worked for the Palestinian National Authority (2005 for 6 months).

22 – Shot in arm. Unable to work. (Received government pension for 6 years.)

23 –

24 –

25 –

26 –

27 –

28 –

29 – Left Gaza forever (3rd May 2013).

– Taxi to Cairo, Egypt (1 night stay). Bought plane ticket to Indonesia for \$700.

– Flew to Doha, Qatar (1 night transit).

– Arrived Jakarta and travelled through Indonesia. Drove through forests to a secret beach location (1 week).

– Sailed with 150 people on a fishing boat (6 days). Six days at sea – no food or water during the last 4 days. Boat started sinking.

– Arrived Christmas Island Immigration Detention Centre (stayed 6 weeks).

– Transferred to Curtin Immigration Detention Centre, Western Australia (1 week).

– Released into the Australian community (11th July 2013).

30 – Celebrated my 30th Birthday in Darwin (27th May 2014).

31 – Moved from Darwin to Sydney (30th May 2015).

Welcome

"Hello," said a soft, sweet voice.

"You help refugees?" the voice of a tall, dark stranger with bright brown eyes continued. He was standing behind the counter of a Red Cross Charity Shop. His eyes gleamed as he scrutinised my dark blue uniform.

"Yes, I am a psychologist and I help refugees," I said smirking to myself at his boldness to ask.

"I am refugee!" said the man.

"My parents were refugees too," I responded.

And that is how I met Raed Zanoon.

Raed is a 30-year-old Palestinian refugee from the Gaza Strip, a small crescent of coast in the Middle East that has been embroiled in terrible violence for decades. The Department of Immigration and Border Protection granted Raed a Temporary Safe Haven (Subclass 449) Visa in Australia on 11 July 2013. But by the time I met Raed in Darwin a few months later, he was already a popular community figure. Working as a volunteer at the Red Cross, Raed has spent most days sorting, hanging, ironing, and selling pre-loved clothes to raise money for charity. As for Raed's cooking, well – that was a real surprise. Although traditional Arabic culture tends to keep men out of the kitchen, Raed has proved himself to be a "Middle East Master Chef". In any case, Raed and I quickly became friends. After all, he was a refugee and I helped refugees. He was the son of refugees – and I was a daughter of refugees. He lived near the Middle East and I am East European, and so on.

Soon after meeting Raed, I visited his home in Darwin. It wasn't the best accommodation for a newcomer to Australia. Sure, the two-bedroom unit was tidy, large and clean. But it was lonely and expensive. When Raed moved in, he was sleeping on a tile floor in a room that had no bed or any furniture at all. He felt so alone there that he couldn't sleep at night and his nightmares got worse. He was living with people who didn't even talk to him. Hardest of all, Raed was receiving a Red Cross allowance of around $225 a week but he was paying $200 a week rent. That left Raed with just $25 a week for food, medicine, clothes, bus fare, emergencies, and everything else he needed. I found Raed a cheaper and better place in Darwin and bought him some furniture – a bed, a small table, chair, floral curtains, a rug, and lots of cushions. Raed liked the carpet and cushions the most. "This is how Arab people sit together," he told me. After living there for a while with a few housemates, including other refugees, Raed didn't feel so alone anymore in this big, brown, sunburnt country.

It was not long before I noticed Raed's Gazan 'get-up-and-go'. Raed was very creative – constantly coming up with good ideas. "Julie-Anne, why don't you do this... ?" and, "Julie-Anne, why don't you do that... ?" Raed was also very kind – cooking people meals and helping agencies with charity events. In particular, I noticed community values were important to Raed. When he cooked, he cooked for everyone. And it didn't matter if you had eaten or not. "Come on, food ready, come and eat please!" he announces to this day. There's a mad rush to the table because everyone is so keen to taste his delicious Gazan dishes. What's more, Raed loved telling stories. He would talk about his family, life in Palestine, the Gaza War, his worries, dreams and more.

At this time in Australian history, the processing of refugees is a hot current affair at the centre of international attention. This makes Raed's story totally important and timely. Whilst Raed is grateful to live in a country where there is no war, no terrorists stalking him with machine guns, the Government's "No Advantage Policy" is considered a dark mark in Australia's immigration history. Many academics, lawyers, and health experts say that current immigration policies are harsh and inhumane. Even worse, more disturbing dangers might lie ahead for Raed – and for all of us. After all, some Australians seem to *hate* refugees, especially the ones who come here by boat. "Stop the boats," politicians campaign. "Let them drown," a chorus of Aussie voices follows. How healthy and helpful is this attitude? Who does it really hurt? As debate about asylum seekers peaks, Raed's story washes up on our shores tackling the biggest questions asked about "boat people" today:

Why did Raed leave his country to come to Australia?

How did he get here? Why did he come by boat?

What do refugees like Raed want here?

If refugees live in Australia, what does this country lose? Gain?

How does the refugee hate debate affect society? People like us?

Can refugees like Raed *really* achieve the happiness, freedom and peace they are seeking? That they have always dreamed about? That they risked their lives for?

Not only will Raed's exciting true life story increase your insight into these important issues, you will also get an insider's look into a top secret world that few have seen – *daily life inside the deadly and dangerous Gaza Strip from a 'local's' point of view.* Further, Raed's story is instructive: it reveals powerful survival skills. Whoever you are – rich or poor, young or old, man or woman, Indigenous-Australian, a Settler from a distant land, or recently arrived Refugee – you are bound to find rich treasure from Raed's journey across the sea.

The idea of capturing Raed's exciting story in a book was both of ours. But the story is Raed's – seen through his eyes. Since Raed's English is not fluent, I merge Raed's experiences with my writing style to bring his story to life. Given that Raed left and risked everything to come here by boat, if his story helps to:

- Describe current affairs in a way that advances society
- Bring people closer together
- Promote peace
- Inspire you to follow your dreams, no matter what well then, Raed the refugee emerges as an 'ambassador for humanity' bearing a bright message of hope that can only "advantage" you, me, Australia – and the world.

– Dr Julie-Anne Sykley

Trapped

Day after day, day after day,
We stuck, nor breath nor motion;
As idle as a painted ship
Upon a painted ocean.
– Samuel Taylor Coleridge (1772–1834)

I notice the hot air hanging heavily around me.

It alludes to more humid weather ahead as does the cloudy horizon.

This tropical climate is choking me now and wearing down our boat.

Today is the 15th of May 2013 and I am in deep, dark trouble.

A quick scan of the sea supports my growing fears. The waves are low and grey, the tide steady and strong, and slow vulture-ish currents circle beneath the steely surface of the water. The sea has cruel plans for me today. I sit on the edge of the wooden boat and watch the waves troll by. My muscles tense every time our boat tilts even a little. At this moment the atmosphere is so thick I cannot breathe. It is as if the ocean is trying to kill me… silently, stealthily, slowly. Of course, my racing thoughts just make my sense of dread worse. I shudder with fear.

I have always tried to be a good person, a good Arab, a good 'Gazan'. But my life has not been easy. All I have ever wanted is to be happy, healthy, and free. But this is not possible where I come from: the Gaza Strip in Palestine – the 'valley of death'. This part of the world is ripped apart by war and terrorism. The fighting is fierce, disturbing, and constant. There, I have seen enough hunger, hatred, death and despair to make my night-mares live on forever. So I had to flee the deadly Gaza Strip just to stay alive. Now I fear for my life all over again as I sink in eerie silence into the sea.

Our fishing boat is just a tiny blue speck – if that – floating on a still, dull surface known as the Indian Ocean. I'm sure we haven't moved an inch for the past five days. It is like I am stuck inside a painting, condemned forever in grey. As a poor and simple man, what match am I against the forces of nature or angry sea gods? What chances do I have of surviving this endless stretch of open empty water? Nevertheless, due to a mix of choice and chance, I am here. Trapped at sea. About to rest at the bottom of a liquid tomb. The sea looks keen to swallow and stew all 150 of us today – men, women, children and babies – all crammed together tightly on a boat. "Why?" I sob. "Why me? Why this?" I ask myself. I do not know how to answer. Deep down in my heart, however, I know that the boat will not stay afloat for much longer. Soon, I will drown.

It is true that your whole life comes to mind just before you die. The day I thought I would drown, thoughts and feelings – good and bad, happy and sad, words and pictures – all these appeared vividly inside my head. My life movie, made with sights and sounds from the past, just kept drawing me deeper and deeper inside myself. For instance, I saw my mother's bright brown eyes gazing down at me kindly, warmly, with love. I saw, very clearly, the dear faces of all my brothers and sisters too. Especially Amjad, my favourite brother. Amjad's bronze cheeks and big white grin glowed as he nursed me back to health with water, medicine and stupid jokes just after I was shot in Gaza. Then, I could hear Amjad screaming loudly in his sleep, which he often did long after the Hamas Terrorists in Palestine released him from their brutal prison. Other images lit up my mind. I will never forget the orange glow of Gaza as it fell to the ground in fire and flames after Israeli forces bombed Palestine. Sometimes the most horrific memories of all would play out in my head. A Hamas soldier dressed in black would be standing right in front of me and pointing his gun into my face. Then headless people and half-bodies flashed through my mind. An arm here, legs there, red blood pooling on a concrete floor. Choke! I feel sick. I want to vomit, but I can't. I have had no food and water for days, so my shrivelled stomach is useless.

More recent memories are dim, obscure, unclear. My trip to Indonesia just a few days ago invokes strange shapes and sinister ideas. I must be remembering the people-smuggling trade. This underground business is so dodgy, you never know what people will do to you. Or what will happen in the future. Will you get that boat ride you paid for? Will you get to your destination safely? Or will the smugglers just steal your money and leave you lost in Asia somewhere? Sometimes, not knowing your future or wondering whether you will make it out alive or not from the jungles of Jakarta is far worse than the sure hell you are trying to flee. After a while, my life story fades away. I have had no food, no water, no shade, no sleep… for how many days now? It doesn't really matter anymore. I am too tired to care, too weak to go on.

As night falls, our little boat sinks deeper, and I can feel it moving down into the dark, warm water, inch by painful inch. What do you think about when you are going to die? Now I know. I glance up at the sky and smile. Throughout my whole journey, I have talked so much to God already:

"God?" I say, gazing at the lovely night, searching the black sky above.

"I am sorry, God," I say. Salty tears dribble down towards my cracked lips. Or maybe it was sea spray, or Heaven crying, or all of these. My miserable thoughts continue:

"If I die, please God, forgive me.

Maybe you can give me a life in Heaven.

I have already lost my life in Gaza, you understand?

I lost my childhood. I lost my freedom. I lost the chance to have a good life.

I lost my country, my home, my family and my friends.

I lost *everything* in Palestine because of war.
Why did I leave everything I know and love behind me?
Because I am looking for peace.
I – just – want – peace."

Shadows beneath the surface of the water swirl more greedily now. But my worst enemy has stalked me all along. There, deep inside my brooding mind, my saddest thoughts start to torture me. In a fleeting moment of weakness, the darkest thought rip grabs me. My most chilling ideas pull me under... drowning me in despair. My body is already so tired that I don't feel like fighting anymore. Well then, why not? Why not stop the pain?

For a moment, the thought of being wrapped inside a warm wreath of seawater makes the idea of death enticing and exciting in a way:

"I think it is better if I die, God."

The relief is instant.

I feel a huge weight lift off my shoulders... off my heart.

"I am a failure, God.

I have failed as a man and as the oldest son in my family," I moan.

"I have never looked after my family properly. And now, I will never be able to help them. Why? Because I am going to die in this stupid ocean!" I continue, sobbing more strongly now. "Look at me, I am crying like a baby – so unlike the man I have always wanted to be. I am not good enough for this world. I am no good to anyone at all," I sigh heavily.

"I am sorry, Mum, God, everyone! Sorry, sorry, sorry for everything!"

All of a sudden, the guilt that has weighed me down my whole life detaches itself. My heart breaks, the floodgates open, my tears gush forth. I drown in a sea of my own emotional anguish. Everything that has ever unsettled me finally escapes...

What is that strange sound? I can hear scores of soft sighs rushing out of places in my body where my saddest secrets have cut me. An invisible force seems to be escaping from my deepest emotional wounds. Is this my soul departing my body? I look up at the night sky for the last time. A silver moon and bright stars hang above me in the darkness. Now I am getting so tired that I close my eyes. I slip into sleep, a misty mental state. The end is very near now – and so glorious. Aaah! My subconscious mind digs up my best life memories for the last time. What's more, my sweetest moments do not appear as words or images – they pour out in the oldest and most universal language known to humankind – as emotions from my heart and as pure energy from my soul – in the form of love! Yes! I am *feeling* the happiest times of my life… my mother's laughter… the first time I saw my wife's face… the moments my sons were born… I immerse myself in this inexplicable bliss, in this positive energy – in all this *love*. Then I float away… above the busy physical world. I am on my way to meet the others, for sure. After all, I have been searching for peace all my life. And now, I am almost there, near the brilliant light ahead of me. I am entering a heavenly plane, a mysterious new world, a place that feels like an Arabian dream.

Arabian Nights

Hidden Treasure

I do not know where I am. I don't even know if I am dead or alive. All I know now is that I am recalling a beautiful memory. My mind has focussed its attention on a dreamy place. I am sitting on a lovely beach somewhere in Gaza. In fact, the Gaza Strip is located in an extraordinary place: at the juncture of Africa and Asia. As such, the coast of Palestine is paradise. It boasts beautiful beaches, tasty seafood, and archaeological treasure. If it wasn't for war and terrorism in my home country, life would be great here. I know that Gaza – the gateway to Asia – has always been a busy trading port and cultural centre for thousands of years. Alexander the Great conquered Gaza in 332 BCE. Then it was ruled by the Romans, becoming part of the Islamic Empire later on. The Crusaders and the Ottomans invaded Gaza after that. Even the French Conqueror Napoleon Bonaparte visited Palestine in 1799. During the First World War, Gaza was a famous battle zone. These days – in my lifetime, that is – this exotic slice of coast has become one of the deadliest and most notorious war zones in the world.

Despite ongoing war, I am proud of my city's rich history and culture. For example, Gaza's oldest, largest and most famous Mosque is the Grand Omari Mosque. It began as a Roman temple, which was later turned into a church. With the arrival of Islam, this building was restored in the seventh century as a Mosque. Inside, a giant courtyard comprises mazes, gardens, and marble columns, which give this holy place the prestige of a grand palace. It is no wonder this building was a source of my childhood fantasies. Whenever I roamed here, I could easily imagine myself ruling Gaza peacefully as a King, or maybe marrying a beautiful woman, or hosting huge feasts for the people of Gaza. One of the oldest gold markets in the world –

Souq Dahab – still trades nearby. I explored this market in my younger years, hoping to find a magic lamp with a genie inside. In the North of Gaza lie Byzantine ruins and tombs, adding a Slavic touch here. In addition, I have never been bored gazing at Gaza's architecture and mosaic designs – they are intricate and stunning. There are also many Islamic galleries selling embroidery, rugs, pottery, metals, and art. Meanwhile, the city streets flaunt graffiti. Our public street art shows what is really on our minds and what really hurts us. Here are numerous images of war, mainly rockets, since this is the weapon of choice in Gaza-Israel battles. The big billboards always remind me that since rocket attacks began in June 2004, several thousand Palestinians in Gaza have been killed by Israeli forces. Again, my Gaza stirs up feelings of pain inside me.

To lessen my mental suffering, my mind diverts me to the main road of Gaza called Omar Almoukhtar Street. This tree-lined street cuts through the busiest parts of Gaza where malls, shops, hotels, banks and parks cheer up the city. An Alfinak bird statue marks the city centre to honour the lives of Palestinians who have died in the Gaza War. Many times I have wandered these streets, sometimes in the shade of the huge trees that grow here, where I would reflect upon all the innocent Palestinian people who lost their lives to war. Omar Almoukhtar Street is so long that it divides Gaza from the east right across to the west by the sea. Who would imagine that this street leads to some of the most famous beaches in the world? Indeed, not only is Gaza's best kept secret its beaches, enjoying yourself at the beach is a choice survival skill in Gaza. Visiting the beach is one of the best ways to escape the violence, chaos and conflict that pervade the Gaza Strip of Death.

Beach Fantasy

When I visit the sea and gaze at the beautiful ocean, I feel free. I can forget about my problems, my poverty, and the bombs for a while. At the beach, I don't think so much about our lives ruined by war and terrorism, or about the high walls and road blockades that trap us here. When I stand at the ocean's edge, breathe in the sea breeze, and stare at the blue horizon, my soul feels alive again. The pretty Palestinian coast helps me to think more positively about the future. In some places, seaweed sticks to dark rocks. This makes the colour of the water change from clear aqua to dark green to black, which changes my outlook too. If someone takes a camel for a stroll along the sand or bathes a magnificent Arabian horse at the water's edge, the beach becomes extra enchanting. Not even war can destroy the wonderful way the Gazan coast makes me feel.

My favourite time to visit the sea is just after the sun sets, the daylight dies, and the busy crowds go home. Here, at the edge of the Mediterranean Sea, the white shores and cliffs plunge into the colourful water. Here, the gold sand turns to beige and blue water darkens to violet. Meanwhile, the green palms transform into black silhouettes that guard the crimson sky. It is at this time that my Gazan beach comes alive with night magic. It signals the onset of dark delights that I am yet to experience. As the seaside takes on a more entrancing mood, I can dream, imagine possibilities, and think about beautiful things more easily.

On some nights at the beach, my friends, cousins, younger brother Ayman and I would visit the beach and build a fire on the sand. "What are we eating tonight?" I would ask our group. "Chicken," they would frequently answer. We would dig a hole in the sand to light a fire and then bake chicken in the hot burning coals. Before that, we would have washed the chicken wings in lemon juice at home. This makes the meat clean and white. A sprinkle of herbs and spices adds flavour – garlic, turmeric, chilli and curry give this meal a delicious taste. As we wait for the food to finish cooking, we play music or just sit on the sand and chat.

I remember one night we decided to go for a swim as the food was taking longer to cook than expected. All of us were wearing shorts and we entered the warm water. The sea felt so good against my skin after a hot day in Gaza. We walked further and further into the Mediterranean Sea. Swimming in the black water under a silver moon, when the cliffs all around you glow white, is magic. Once my brother Ayman started splashing me with water. So I swam up to him and splashed him back. We splash each other so much we are drenched – laughing and joking with each other the whole time. After all that swimming and splashing, we suddenly realise that the chicken is still cooking in the fire. "I hope it's not burnt!" I shout to the others. On hearing this, the group rushes out of the water. You see, I was very hungry and I was just trying to get everyone to head back to the ground oven. At last the food is cooked. We all sit down on the sand to eat our Gazan-style charcoal chicken – crunchy black coating outside, juicy meat inside. It tastes delicious. After that, fresh pieces of fruit and Arabic-style tea. "Anyone for chai [tea]?" After dinner we sit on the sand, play cards, listen to more music or just watch the waves roll back and forth.

It is always a perfect night – visiting nature, sitting on the sand, and relaxing in a Palestinian paradise with friends. Sometimes the starlight glittered so brightly that it lit up the edge of the dark bay that curved around the beach. This formed a winding silver road that stretched far along the coast, far along the sands of time, through dreams and desires, leading somewhere into the infinite. When the mood was serene, my thoughts were really calm, and my heartbeat slowed right down, my mind wandered a lot. I often imagined that if I was a magician, I could just walk across the top of the water to a land far away, into a free country perhaps, and just live there forever in peace.

Out of the Blue

As long as the bright moon keeps floating across the dark sky, my Arabian dream drifts on. I am lying on my back, relaxing deeply, listening to the waves caress the shore. Then I hear to my surprise the sound of boats purring in the distance. Their rumbling motors grow louder and louder as they approach my tranquil seaside retreat. The sound starts to break up my beautiful trance, my dreamy Arabian night. "Boats! Damn it!" I mutter to myself. "How rude of them to interrupt my beach fantasy!" Although I am tired after a long, hot day outside, I focus my attention on the increasing volume of the motors. Now I am more awake. I open my eyes slowly and look up. I see a beautiful moon and stars hanging above me in the night sky. It is the scene from my Arabian dream. *Wh– ?!* It is also the same scene I saw when I fell asleep in my little fishing boat! All of a sudden, it hits me hard. I see water all around me. I am so disappointed. I am not on a beautiful beach in Gaza at all. Reality sinks in more. Where am I? I am still stranded in the middle of the ocean on a rickety, old boat. Suddenly, a dark shape appears in the water. Its quick movement startles me. A shot of adrenaline jumpstarts my heart. I am wide awake now for sure! Oh my God! I am in danger! All around the boat sharks are swimming! Their pointy fins stick out, slicing the smooth surface of the water like razors. Terror rips through me as I imagine one of the sharks eating me if I fall in. Now that I am completely alert, I glance around quickly to see where the motor noise is coming from. I look behind me and see two dots growing bigger and bigger as they advance. I rub my eyes, focus my gaze and look again. They are boats – foreign vessels! My prayers have been answered! "*YES!*" I shout with joy. "The Australian Navy has come to rescue us!"

I am so happy now that the Australian Navy is here. For the first time since leaving Gaza, I feel safe. When the navy officers survey us, they do not look angry; they smile. After living in a war zone my whole life, I cannot believe that these officers aren't angry at us. They tell us they came because they noticed our boat drifting from a distance, and it looked like we were in trouble. They didn't come to kill us, they came to *help* everyone on the boat. The crew seemed truly happy to see us all, relieved that we were all alive. The first thing a senior navy officer asks us is how many babies and children are on board the vessel. "Seven are on board!" a voice in the darkness shouts back. The officer leaves us for a short while. When he comes back, he brings with him milk for all the babies and water for everyone on board. I glance around at my shipmates and for the first time since we boarded the boat in Indonesia, everyone is smiling and happy. Everyone receives a bottle of water from the navy officers. When it is my turn to get some water from the officer, I just look up at him. "Thank you," I say, with a big smile on my face.

The officer just smiles back in reply.

After everyone receives their water, the navy gives everybody a number. We are then told to wait for orders from the navy boss about what to do next. A short time later, the navy officer returns.

"Everybody – you all need to go back to Indonesia!" the officer says.

What?!

After hearing this, my shipmates burst into tears.

I can't hold back my own tears. *"We can't go back to our countries,"* I think to myself.

"Our lives are in great danger there.

We have no passports, no money, no nothing."

"I left my family, I left everything behind to come to a peaceful country," a voice from the gloom shouts out.

"A terrorist wants to shoot me, kill me, maybe torture me in jail first!" cries another.

It feels as if all hope has been extinguished in my weak body forever. I start to fall apart.

"If I die here, it is better than returning back to Gaza," I say to myself.

At this point in time, I just want to jump off the boat and finish my life.

"If I am forced to go back, just to be gunned down and murdered in Gaza, then – yes – I would rather die here in the sea," I decide determinedly. My death wish is strong, very strong. But when I think of my mother, I don't throw myself overboard right there and then because I know it would destroy her. I promised her I would stay safe. So I keep my promise. I delay the urge to kill myself for just a brief moment. I open my mind to see what will happen next.

Some people start crying and screaming, "If I go back to my country, I will be killed!"

"We will die!" everyone cries. After a while, everybody starts shouting, "NO! NO! NO!" to the navy.

"We don't want to go back! We *can't* go back! How can we go back? We have no homes, no safety, no future. We have nothing!" The senior navy officer leaves us once again in the darkness. Again, I am trapped. We are all trapped. Not just trapped because we are lost in the middle of the ocean. We are trapped to relive the horror of our pasts. Trapped in a dark unknown, our future directions uncertain. We are petrified, too scared to breathe. We wait – more lifelessly than marine fossils fixed in rock – for the result of a 'phone call' that will change our lives forever, that our lives literally depend on. After we wait a while at this turning point, the navy officer returns with the news: "I've just received a call telling us to take everyone to Christmas Island," he reports.

We can't believe it!

We all suddenly feel alive again!

We jump, we cheer, we cry, we are so happy!

The navy officers start taking us, five at a time, on to small boats and then transporting us on to a larger ship. I climb on board the huge sailing vessel, and then the navy doctor checks us all to see if anyone is really sick.

It feels fantastic to be finally on board a large Australian naval ship. We are safe and sound at last. Then we eat our first meal for days – tuna and rice, and it is so delicious. I really wanted to thank the person who made that meal for us, especially as it was my first time trying Australian food. Sitting on top of the open deck, we are shaded by large umbrellas to protect us from the sun. A gentle breeze blows through my hair as we cruise through the water. After living in terror every day in the Gaza Strip for 29 years, after dreaming about freedom and peace for so long, and after admitting to myself that I would be leaving behind my Arabian nights forever, I head for Christmas Island.

Rafah Backstreets (2003)

All my life I dreamed of living in peace. Now that I am on the other side of the world, it is hard to get used to the idea that I am finally here. Although arriving on Christmas Island is one of the most exciting times of my life, it was also one of the scariest. My life becomes strange, surreal, and stressful. Not only was I in a new country, but one full of very weird things like large birds that cannot fly, but run faster than kangaroos. There are also parrots with no colour – white cockatoos and black ones. Add to that a host of fatally poisonous insects, spiders and snakes, and I can't help but wonder: "Where have I ended up? A deadly zoo?" I start to notice that whenever I am tired, missing my family, worrying about the future, or unable to sleep at night because of headaches, nightmares, panic attacks, pain in my arm, or other problems, my mind becomes a time machine. It sends me back through time, back into my own personal history because that is the only familiar thing to me in this crazy, new world. In my first few days on Christmas Island, my attention sends me back to Gaza. My mind, maybe in an attempt to protect me, urges me to review and relive my early life. Back there, in the foggy mists of time, I retrace old steps, reunite with forgotten memories, and explore the dark and distant landscapes of my past.

Early Life

I was born a refugee on the 27th of May 1984 inside the Rafah Refugee Camp in Palestine. My birthplace is best known as the Gaza Strip. My father's name is Abdul Hakim Zanoon and my mother's name is Alia. Just like me, both my parents are refugees too. In fact, my entire family are refugees. You see, my family originally came from Yafa, Palestine. This area later became Occupied Palestine. My grandfather had to leave his Yafa home about half a century ago because of the Nakba (Disaster). That's when over 700,000 Palestinian Arabs were evicted from their homes and forced to leave their lands. During the 1947–1948 Civil War in Palestine, people needed to flee to anywhere it was considered safe at the time. From Jordan to Syria and beyond, we Palestinians were scattered across the wide Arabic Peninsular. Later, a mandatory law was passed forbidding Palestinian people from returning to their homes and lands. And that is why and how my family and I ended up in Gaza as refugees.

I came from a very poor family. My father was unemployed most of his life because there was no work in Gaza. Gaza is a war zone, rife with power cuts, unclean water, poverty and lack of work. This means no money for food – and dirty, dangerous living conditions. As a result, my father became a very sick and angry man. In fact, Abdul was so traumatised by the brutal violence he witnessed in Gaza that he would have terrible temper tantrums. Sometimes he would fly into uncontrollable rages and just smash the house and furniture to pieces. Worse, he would beat up the family or throw pots and pans at my head if I didn't have enough money to buy him cigarettes. My father would often scream at the top of his voice: "Allah Yalan Hamas! [God curse the Hamas!]" At other times, when Abdul was calm, he would just sit on a dirty old mattress outside our house in the dust and eat oranges. He threw spiralled strips of citrus peel all around himself. This made my dad look like a great ruler of an orange-coloured kingdom. It also increased the large amount of rubbish already piling up in the street.

The hard life in Gaza also affected my mother. Alia had no family in Gaza. She was orphaned when she was just a teenage girl. Despite this, my mother forged herself into a resilient and resourceful matriarch. She cared deeply for all of us, made sure she had food for everyone, and she kept the family together. Alia prayed and prayed to Allah, the all-powerful Islam God, for help. And even though help never came, I think that my mum's belief in a higher spiritual power kept her soul safe, intact and pure. Every morning, my mum delighted in waking me up to feed me. She would say: "Allah yahfazk, habibi [God bless you, darling]," and also "Arjuk ehda shuye [Please be calm]." I have cherished my mum's precious words to this day. In fact, during the hardest and darkest times of my life, my mum's messages often re-emerged as my brightest rays of hope. You see, although I was shot, saw people die in front of me, and although I am a poorly educated man who has never had a professional job, one thing I have had and always will have is my mother's special message. It soothes me to this day whenever I need it: "Edha, ehda. Koun andac salam [Stay calm. Have peace in your heart]."

Altogether, my parents Abdul and Alia had 13 children. That might seem like a lot of children but this is normal in Gaza. More children mean more chance of the family surviving. If a parent or parents are killed (the risk of getting bombed or executed in Gaza is very high), then an older sibling becomes head of the house. Since the younger and more vulnerable children have someone older to look after them, the little ones don't perish. What is also normal in Gaza is that very large families like ours live in very small houses. Our family home had three rooms: a small bathroom, a bedroom for my parents, and a kitchen where we cooked and all the children bunked down for the night. It wasn't an ideal situation but we made the best of it as it was all we had. Of course, we were always grateful to have each other.

The first child born into the Zanoon clan was a girl, Izdhar. When she was aged five and I was three, we were walking together to the shop to buy some sweets. A car ran her over in the street. I was with her when she died but I don't remember that. The second child to join our family was Amira (a girl) and then me. As the eldest boy in an Arab family, I am second in charge (after my dad) for looking after my family. Next came Izdhar2 (girl), Ayman (boy), Achraf (boy), Anhar (girl), Amjad (boy), Adham (boy), Inas (girl), Abdulla (boy), Saddam (boy) and finally, our lucky thirteenth: Nada, my baby sister who is still not even 5 years old. The older siblings – Amira, Izdhar2 and Ayman – are married. The others are not married because life in Gaza is too hard and they are too poor. What's more, life is far too dangerous these days.

Deep inside the Gaza Strip, life is hard for all families. Every morning at 4am Islamic scripture resounds loudly on the loud speakers. Of course, this wakes everybody up. Then the roosters start to crow, the dogs start to bark, and children start to fight, laugh, scream and play barefoot in the streets. After that, you can hear the sound of people walking by and motorcycles zipping past. But the grocery sellers are the worst. One after the other, men would stroll underneath my window, or ride bicycle-driven carts full of vegetable wares, waking me up with their deafening announcements on megaphones and microphones: "Tomatoes! Tomatoes for sale!" a loud voice would boom. "Melons, water-melons – very cheap – only one shekel a kilo!" another noisy grocer might shout. Such raucous marketeering every morning drove me crazy! Sometimes I would get so annoyed that I would open my upstairs window, get a large bottle, fill it with cold water, and pour water all over the people yelling in the street below. After a brief bout of cursing and swearing, the aggrieved and wet sellers would leave. But then, barely a few moments later, another seller with a loudspeaker would come along and disturb my sleep. My silent victory would never last for long. In the last seven years that I lived in Gaza, I tried to stay in bed for as long as possible to get up as late as possible. You see, after I was shot in the arm by a terrorist, I couldn't work due to my significant physical disability. At night, I couldn't sleep due to all the pain. My daily routine went something like this. At around midday, I would get up, shower, dress, eat fava beans, chickpeas, or kishta (cow milk) with pita bread, or whatever was available at home. Then I would go and visit my dear paternal grand-mother Aziza. We would sit together sipping black Arabic tea (flavoured with fresh sage or mint leaves) and have long talks about Palestine, the old days, and the peaceful life before Israel occupied Palestine. After I finished visiting my grandmother, I would return home and relax on a mattress in the street outside my home. I liked to greet people passing by with "Salam Alekom [Peace to you]." During my final years of life inside Gaza, no one in my family worked. Why? Because there was no work. Because of violence, terrorism, and war. Our whole family was trying to survive on a small United Nations war pension in the end.

Unlike me, my mum Alia was a real early bird. She woke up at 5am each morning and prayed indoors. Then she got the younger children ready for school. She often made falafel sandwiches with tomato and lettuce for the children's school lunch. Afterwards, every evening at the end of the day, we would all meet together again as a family. At night, my mum cooked dinner for everyone. We often ate hommos, falafel, salad, fried potato chips, and omelettes. But our Arabic menu did not include meat; that was far too expensive – an utter luxury. After eating, we would drink cool water or hot Arab chai. On very rare occasions, if we had any money to spare, my mum would make delicious Palestinian desserts. My favourite sweet was gata'ef – fried pastry dumplings filled with dates and shredded coconut, and infused with honey. After my sisters washed the dinner dishes, we would relax as a family in the house. If we were lucky enough to have electricity, we would sink back into the soft cushions and snuggle next to each other to watch television programs like *Bab Al-Hara* [The Neighbourhood's Gate]. Watched by tens of millions of viewers from poor Palestine to the affluent cities of the Persian Gulf, this Syrian soap opera is the world's favourite Arabic television series (about a pharmacist's family during the 1930s war era). But on other nights we had no electricity. The Hamas Terrorists cut it off. On those occasions when there was no power, no problem. We would dine as a family by candlelight and chat and joke over chai or freshly squeezed fruit juice. Sometimes I would use that poor, dim lighting to my advantage. If I was really hungry, or hadn't eaten much that day, I would sneak an extra piece of food into my belly without being caught.

I know that on the outside (and especially to outsiders) the Gaza Strip must look like a poor society, a ghetto full of people with no purpose and pathetic lives. Besieged by violence, rubbish and rubble, Gaza might seem barren, ugly, and miserable on the surface. But as a local, I can assure you that on the inside Gaza is a very different world. It can be a rich and powerful psychological place. Beneath Gaza's crushing conditions, many residents are strong and beautiful. People such as my mum exemplify "sumud". This Arabic word means "steadfast perseverance" and it promotes Palestinian resilience. I have seen many ordinary sumuds in Rafah rebuild their houses and their lives despite the intrusion of the Israeli army and military enemies. It is no simple feat to salvage goods from garbage whilst listening to gunfire and dodging explosions all around you, to risk your life just to obtain a few simple necessities. Resourcefulness is a big survival skill – a hallmark of Gazan character. What's more, I want you to know that, deep down, Gazans are warm and kind people. Just like my parents did and they still do, I am always happy to help others, welcome guests into my home, share what meagre supplies I have, and chat about anything – war, the weather, culture, music, romance, and more.

I think the most important life lesson my mother taught me was to forgive and forget bad people, to live peacefully with others, and to love everyone. This way, you get to experience inner peace. "It's fine, Raed," my mum would often say. "Many people have been through a lot in life and have become unwell. Please be calm and happy, son." "Shukran, Mama [Thank you, Mum]," I would say, looking into her bright brown eyes, and feeling much calmer and happier inside. Sometimes, however, when I rested alone in my bed at night, and heard the guns fire, the missiles whistle, the F-16s fly overhead, and the bombs explode – and the pain in my arm throbbed so badly that I couldn't sleep at all – I would mutter miserably to myself: "Sorry, Mum. It is not easy to forgive and forget cruel people and bad events here... deep inside the Gaza Strip of Death."

Easy Prey

In April 2003 I started working in a clothes shop with Hussein, my younger cousin. Hussein was my dearest cousin and closest friend. Everyone loved Hussein. He walked tall, proud, and had a good-looking body, as if he went to the gym every day. But he didn't. His slim and athletic build was due to all the hard physical work he always did. I felt really sorry for Hussein. His mother died giving birth to him, leaving him an orphan. But Hussein wasn't dear to me because I felt sorry for him. I loved Hussein because he always tried to be happy and positive no matter what. Hussein had a big heart and he always helped others.

Every day Hussein and I worked in a busy clothing shop in Rafah tucked away in a backstreet just behind the UNRWA (United Nations Relief Works Agency). This centre supports the welfare of Palestinian refugees in the Near East. We worked from seven in the morning until seven at night selling cheap clothes imported from China by the shop's owner. The workdays were long and hard in summer. These hotter months drained you of all your energy in no time at all. But despite the heat, we kept working – tired and sweaty – because we needed the money to buy food. Some evenings after work, Hussein and I went for walks to discuss the day or we sat and chatted about what we wanted to do in our lives. Occasionally we visited a little local street café where we would order meat kebabs. Eating meat always made me feel strong and manly, because we rarely could afford it.

When we were feeling energetic, Hussein and I travelled to

other parts of Gaza to buy extra clothes to sell in the store. On Friday nights we sold clothes at the local market to try to make a little extra cash. At the end of the evening shift, we would always split our earnings in half.

"What are you going to do with your share of the money, Hussein?" I asked my cousin once.

"I want to save it all so that when I find a good woman, I can get married. What about you?"

"I am the same as you, Hussein. I think it is time I got married and had a family. It would be really nice to share my life with someone, to feel a warm pair of arms hold me at night."

"Hey, maybe we could get married at the same time, Raed?" my cousin suggested once, smiling widely.

"That would be really good," I replied. This made both of us smile and laugh more.

As my cousin Hussein was dear to me, and we always shared everything together, the idea of sharing a wedding day was truly exciting, a dream come true. They were good, happy times.

But when you live in a deadly strip in the Middle East, targeted by powerful enemies, such lovely dreams are bound to be short-lived. And tragically, they were. In Rafah, at the southern end of Gaza, our families had houses situated just two hundred metres from the Egyptian border. This meant that every day and every night we could hear constant shooting and fighting on both sides of the border. Each time a bomb fell, a terrible aftershock followed, which felt as if a shattering earthquake was ripping the ground apart. Entire houses, including Hussein's and mine, shook terribly as the doors and windows rattled from the shocks. As our homes were right next to the Gaza smuggling tunnels (hundreds of long underground tunnels once used to sneak goods from Egypt into Palestine), the tunnels were still the focus of constant air strikes from the Israeli Defence Force. This made life in Gaza very, very dangerous, and the idea of beautiful wives and double weddings doomed – a fool's errand.

One night, on the 20th of April 2003, Hussein and I were chatting and drinking tea at his home after a long, hot day working at the clothes store. Suddenly, we both heard gunfire in the streets outside and a loud whirring of helicopters in the sky. We both rushed outside to see what was happening. Other people ran out into the street too. I overheard some people saying that Israeli soldiers were heading our way with tanks and many weapons. We started imagining the worst, and our hearts raced fast with fear. It was not long before many snipers arrived, perching like hungry hawks on building tops. Hussein and I didn't really understand what was happening at the time – that the Israelis had come to kill us – so we just kept walking down the street. I opened my mouth to ask Hussein, "What do you think is going on here?" But it was already too late. Hussein was lying on the ground, red blood flourishing all over his white cotton shirt. What? I couldn't believe it! A hawk-eyed sniper shot him in the heart – twice! Without thinking anything, without feeling anything, I just grabbed my cousin tightly in my arms. "It's all right, cousin. It's all right. Everything will be fine," I told him, as hopeless tears ran down my cheeks.

After several minutes – a timeless hell for me – an ambulance arrived. I was still sitting on the ground cradling my cousin and crying. The paramedics approached me. They dislodged Hussein's limp body from my arms and slid him on to a stretcher into the waiting vehicle. I couldn't bear to be separated from my cousin. "Can I come in the ambulance with him please?" I desperately asked the paramedics. "Of course," they replied. "Please come here and sit down." I stepped inside the vehicle, sat beside my cousin, and talked to him the whole way to hospital. "Hussein?! Hussein? Talk to me!" But there was no response – silence – nothing. Once we arrived at the hospital, Hussein was rushed to a room where the doctors examined him. I was left standing on a shiny and squeaky-clean hospital floor in the corridor, frozen, unable to move, unable to speak, in a complete state of shock.

My daze was broken by the sound of a man's voice. I guess it was a doctor talking to a member of our family, all of whom had by now arrived.

"I am so sorry," said the doctor, "but Hussein died a short while ago... We did everything we could... I am really sorry for your loss."

We all just sat there and started crying. "If there is anything you need, please do not hesitate to ask me," the doctor said, barely audible over all the loud weeping and wailing. I cried hard for my cousin Hussein. The grief was fierce, painful, strong. I felt as if my broken heart would just burst right out of my chest, fly out, and splatter like a blob of red jelly all over that shiny hospital floor.

"How can anyone – anyone – do this to another human being?" I screamed.

"And why, why, why Hussein? He was such a good man, such a kind friend. Why did he have to die? Everybody in Rafah loved him so very much," I continued to cry miserably. My darling cousin Hussein – my best friend and family – had been stolen from me forever in a cold and cruel act of murder. To this day, I still don't understand why they shot *him*. Why did *he* have to die?

As my family huddled together at the hospital and cried, I dragged my body, still covered in Hussein's blood, across the smooth floor to stand next my cousin's bed. I felt so sad thinking that Hussein would never fulfil his dream of having the wife and family he always wanted. I wish I could turn back time and see my dearest cousin marry the girl of his dreams. But now this will not happen – never, ever. "Hussein, come back to me. I miss you so much. We have always been there for each other, and now it is just me! How am I supposed to live without you and do things without you by my side?!" A large teardrop rolled down my face. Ever so gently, I bent over Hussein's head and kissed the still, warm mouth that would never smile again.

A few days passed by and I resumed work to try and put some normal routine back into my life. The first day back at work was the hardest, especially when all the customers and shopkeepers kept coming up to me and asking: "Hey, Raed, where is Hussein?"

"I am sorry, he was killed a few days ago," I would reply sadly.

All the customers were shocked. Many of the regular customers were very loyal to Hussein. Over and over, I had to explain what happened to my cousin. I was so relieved and happy when the first workday was finally over. It was emotionally exhausting to have everyone asking me about Hussein. Whenever the memories and thoughts about Hussein flooded back to me, so did my river of tears. The pain was too great to bear. At the end of each day, I locked the shop up quickly and rushed home to try and sleep. I found, however, that I couldn't rest at all, not even at home.

Every night, whenever I fell asleep, Hussein visited me. I saw his bleeding heart, his mouth gasping for air, him dying in my mind… over and over and over. Then, out of the darkest shadows in my dreams, the eerie figure of a woman always appeared. She would look at me, her ghostly eyeless face longing sadly for something her heart desired. I sensed a terrible pain; she desperately wanted something she could never have. Suddenly, I recognise this woman. I know her – and I shiver. She is Hussein's future wife, the woman he was destined not to meet, his bride never-to-be. I sit up in my bed with a jolt, wide awake and sweating.

Muslim Bride (2004)

The Meeting

Many people around the world dream of getting married. And we Gazans are no exception. In 2004, I finally saved all the money I needed for a bride's dowry. You see, in Arabic culture, it is traditional for men to save money for a wife. One evening at home, my mum raised the subject of marriage with me:

"Raed?"

"Yes, Mama?"

"Your aunty has a daughter who wants to marry. She is very beautiful and nineteen years old. If you want, I can arrange a visit."

"I would like that, Mama, thank you."

And just like that, my parents arranged a visit the very next day.

In Gaza, the marriage process usually begins with family members of a prospective couple meeting together and checking each other out. If all parties agree, the couple's fathers will negotiate a dowry. Later on, the parties go to court to sign a marriage contract and then they set a date for a formal wedding. From that point, the man and woman who plan to marry are legally bound to one another. The wedding festivities include separate men's and women's parties, as well as a ceremony for everyone on the wedding day.

I was so excited thinking about my first meeting with a beautiful young woman who might be my wife. On the morning of the day we were to meet, I leapt out of bed, showered and dressed, and went straight to the local barber for a haircut and shave. After grooming and pampering myself, I bought nice clothes and cologne for my meeting with the girl and her family. A white shirt, black trousers, and One Man Show cologne seemed appropriate. I returned home, changed into my new clothes, dabbed on my romantic weapon, and headed downstairs to meet my parents.

My father, mother and I went to the family home of Asma, my bride-to-be. When we walked inside the house, my eyes dropped to the floor immediately. I became very shy. I didn't even look at the young lady that I had gone to meet. But out of the corner of my eye, I did. She was a beautiful woman. A pair of dark eyes peered out from beneath her black hajib. They glittered like jewels when she glanced in my direction, studying me carefully, no doubt. I think she liked me because she turned towards her father who nodded and agreed to a marriage. Then I turned to my father who also agreed to the marriage. After our families agreed, our two fathers sat down to discuss the bride's dowry, as this is how families arrange marriages in Gaza. It is Islamic culture. Asma's father nominated a price: "I want two thousand Dinars (about US $3000) for Asma so she can buy gold, clothes, make-up and whatever else she needs." This is a *lot* of money for an average Arabic-speaking family in Palestine. Asma was an expensive bride! "Fine," my father said. "We have this amount of money. We will bring it here tomorrow." *"What?! Wow! I am getting married!"* I thought. This was one of the most exciting moments of my life! I felt so happy now that I would be sharing my life with someone who seemed so nice. In fact, we planned to be legally engaged the next day. I was so happy that I didn't sleep much that night. In fact, I didn't sleep at all.

The Engagement

When I woke up the next morning after a sleepless night, I was still full of life and had a huge smile on my face. Asma and I were about to enter a rite of passage, a doorway to a new level of social and cultural existence. Today we would be engaged. That afternoon my parents and I visited Asma at her home. This time we brought money for the dowry, as well as some drinks and snacks to celebrate our special occasion. We entered the house, my father handed Asma's father the required money, and we all sat down. I glanced across at Asma from the corner of my eye. She looked so beautiful. I placed my hand upon hers and we recited prayers from the *Quran Al Fatiha* to announce our Engagement in accordance with our Sunni Muslim law and religion.

As soon as the last words of our Engagement vows were spoken, I was happy. So were our families and friends. We celebrated with music, talking and eating. Relatives and friends visited the house to congratulate Asma and me on our holy union. When dinner was ready, we all sat down on rugs and pillows together and ate. We put some traditional Islamic music on the CD player. After a night of chatting, drinking, and eating, I walked home with my parents. "I am sooooo happy," I thought to myself. "I am engaged to be married!" The idea excited me. I had never touched a girl before let alone kissed one. (Sexual acts before marriage are strictly forbidden. This is traditional Islamic culture. The ultimate penalty, according to the Quran, is death). Therefore, as a man about to be married, the idea of touching and kissing a woman made my heart race.

The next day after our Engagement party, I went to work. As a future groom and husband-to-be, I had new responsibilities. I had to save money to look after my fiancée and to make a beautiful family home for us. I also had to buy her gifts. Although I started working really long hours, I still visited Asma once a week. The only place I met Asma was at her house because in Islam it is forbidden for a man and woman to go outside together until they are married. Whenever I visited Asma, a family member would chaperone her and sit with us. I always felt happy to see my fiancée, although we still were not allowed to be alone together. As always, Asma's sister, brother or some other relative would be around to ensure that we didn't have any physical contact with each other.

Once I became so frustrated about the lack of physical

intimacy that I mentioned it to my father. As usual, he had a logical answer. "No problem, son," he said, patting me reassuringly on the shoulder. "Just focus on your work for now. You are working to make a beautiful home for yourselves." "Yes, I am working to make a beautiful home," I would repeat to myself. It became my mantra whenever strong romantic thoughts distracted me. I stuck with it – working solidly for more than a year just to save one thousand Jordanian Dinars (currency of Jordan) to buy some bedroom furniture. I estimated it would take a decade to earn enough money to buy furniture for all the other rooms let alone buy or build the house itself! I began thinking that a proper marriage was just a distant dream, not an achievable reality. Once again, I approached my father and again he answered calmly. "No problem, son," he said, patting my shoulder. "I have an idea." My father arranged to have a meeting with Asma's family. He told them, "I would like my son and your daughter to marry soon. I offer to take your daughter from your family home and welcome her to live with us at my home, Insha Allah [God be Willing]." Asma's family agreed to my father's request. It is amazing how quickly things move in Arabic culture. We were to marry the next day. I was relieved! Excited! Shocked! The following morning I woke up very early to buy myself a wedding suit. A friend helped me to pick out clothes fit for a king. A white shirt (with long sleeves), black trousers, and a golden sash for my waist. I was finally getting married and it felt amazing!

The Wedding

The cloudy sky was tinged with blue. It was my wedding day – one of the happiest times of my life. I was so nervous that I couldn't slow my heart down at all. Whilst Asma and I have spent several months getting to know each other, today would the first time I would see Asma without a headscarf covering her face. And tonight – this is the very first time that we would be alone together. The thought of it made my heart thump even faster – as if a herd of wild Arabian horses were galloping inside it. Until now, Asma and I have only been allowed to meet inside her home, where she is always chaperoned by a relative. And now my imagination was running fast. For the first time in ages, I forgot about the Gaza War and the valley of death I live in. My wedding day was filled only with happy thoughts and feelings of love.

In Gaza, it is traditional for the groom's family to host a large wedding dinner for relatives and friends. Two traditional parties are supposed to follow the wedding, one for men and one for women. Women get together at a *henna*, a happy night of singing, dancing, mingling, and friendly chatter. After the formal ceremony, a perfect Gaza wedding might also include a Palestinian folk dance called the "Dabka" (which I know my brother Ayman can dance). Soon after a ceremony called *sacra* occurs, two songs play. One announces the delivery of *somogeeya*, a traditional purple dish from Gaza. The groom's family presents plates of this food to all the wedding guests. The second song thanks guests and wishes them a safe night. Of course, that is a perfect Gazan wedding. As I came from a poor family, our wedding was much simpler. It had no food, no dancing, and no live music. We did not even have a wedding cake because we could not afford it. Never mind, we just made the best of what we did have.

On the morning of my wedding day, my brothers, male cousins and friends borrowed and decorated an old car with flowers and colourful ribbons. Meanwhile, the women spent all morning putting on make-up to make themselves look beautiful. After lunch, the car covered with flowers (a bouquet on wheels) picked Asma up to take her to my uncle's house, where the wedding would take place. I, like every single groom in the world, waited restlessly for my beautiful bride to arrive.

It wasn't long before Asma appeared at the doorway of my

uncle's house. She gracefully entered the room in her wedding dress. She was wearing a long white dress that flowed down her body like a waterfall. A white veil floated down to her silver shoes. Asma's dark brown hair was tied at the back and decorated with a few sparkling stones. Wow! Asma looked like a Gazan goddess. She drifted towards me from the other side of the room, past the white flowers and past the awed faces of the wedding guests. When Asma reached me, her father joined us and handed Asma to me. "Asma is your responsibility now, take good care of her," he told me. "I will," I replied. Under Islam, this is the way of weddings. We sat and relaxed together for a while, waiting for a judge (who has the power to marry people) to arrive from the local courthouse. As Asma stood next to me, my eyes met hers. They were a chocolate colour whilst her eyelids were dusted with gold. When Asma noticed I was gawking at her, her pink lips parted into a sweet smile. At that moment, I was in heaven.

After the official ceremony was finished, I got an empty chair and placed it next to mine at the front of the room so that my new wife could sit next to me. We played Arabic music on the CD player. Everyone mingled, drank tea and soft drinks, and socialised the whole night. When the party finally died down, I reached out to hold my wife's hand in public for the very first time and we strolled home together alone. "Tonight is the first time in my life that I am going to touch or kiss a woman," I thought to myself. When we entered the house, we went upstairs into the bedroom, and sat down on the bed. I kissed my Asma gently, adoringly, passionately on the lips. Then my heart raced wildly as I shut the bedroom door behind me.

The Fight

It did not take long for Asma to change. After just one month of marriage, I felt like she didn't love me at all and never did. How did I know? The signs were clear. Every day when I came home from work she would shout at me, "I hate you! I don't want you!

I hate my family because they made me marry you!" She also started spitting at me. Sometimes she spat in my face because I looked at her and sometimes she complained that I was standing too close. Most of the time it was for no reason at all. When Asma's moods were at their worst, she slapped my face, pinched my arms, or, when she was really angry, she threw hot cups of tea at me. I tried to talk to her, to help her, to settle her. "Habibi [My dear]. What's wrong? Talk to me," I pleaded. But this just made her more angry. Eventually, she didn't even look at me when she stormed out of the house after our arguments. I don't understand why she was like this at all. All I know is that I was really lonely and miserable and that I could not take it for too much longer. Sometimes I wasn't sure which situation was more dangerous. The warring streets of Palestine. Or spending a night at home alone with my wife. My dream bride set my home ablaze with her fiery temper, turning it into a hostile hell, and leaving me burning at the stake. Asma became increasingly abusive over time, both verbally and physically. Our home life became so awful that I had to send Asma back home to her father, "Insha Allah [God Willing]." I eventually approached my father to tell him about my miserable marriage. "Dad, this woman is so bad I don't want her to be in my life anymore. I want to divorce her, Dad." But I didn't, I couldn't.

At that time, I found out that Asma was pregnant with our first child. I was happy that my wife was pregnant but I was certainly not happy with the bad way she was treating me. I tried to be patient. I waited to see if Asma's pregnancy would change her attitude towards me. I secretly hoped and prayed in my heart that the pregnancy would help her, make us close again. But it didn't. It got worse, much worse. Nine argumentative months passed by. Finally, on the 25th of July 2005, our son was born. We named him Jehad and welcomed him into the world. I was over the moon. I couldn't believe that this tiny little boy was *mine*. He was so perfect in every way and so beautiful. Every day I was keen to finish work just to hurry home and hold him.

One day after work, I returned home and was playing with my son as I normally did until it was his bedtime. Then Asma and I headed off to the bedroom so that we could make love, which we still did at times. I started to remove Asma's clothes gradually. When I reached her underwear, I found something. A secret love letter that she wrote to another man and hid inside her pants. I was so upset and angry that I flew into a rage and shouted at her to put her clothes back on. I stormed off to speak to my father. I told him what happened and he listened. Then, he just looked at me and said: "Raed, don't mention this again. Just forget about it." But how could I forget? I felt deeply hurt and betrayed. How could I look at Asma again after she had treated me so unkindly? When she was in love with another man? Under Islam, if a wife or husband has an affair outside marriage, the punishment is death. But I couldn't do that to her and I didn't know how far her affair had gone anyway. All I knew was that I couldn't face her anymore. I had as much as I could take. I trudged back inside the house, walked into the bedroom, and opened the door. Asma was lying casually on the bed painting her nails a different colour as if there was nothing wrong. She didn't even say, "*Sorry.*" "I don't want you here anymore!" I screamed at the top of my voice, just like my father used to scream at me. "You need to leave! Go home! Go back to your family! Get of the house now!" But she didn't, she couldn't.

At that time, I found out that Asma was pregnant again with our second child. This meant she had to stay with me. Again, the months passed by slowly and tension between us grew. Finally, on the 20th of December 2006 my second child was born, another son. We named him Rayan. Despite Asma's hostility towards me, I felt happy inside. When Rayan was born, he was so tiny and looked so helpless and perfect. I felt happy, complete, like a man, having established a proper family. What more could anyone ask? From then on, I worked and worked all the hours I could to provide for my family and be the best husband and father I could be. The work helped to distract me from my growing worries and problems at home. It also kept my mind off the tension, fighting, and warring that was growing stronger outside my home.

Targeted (2006)

As a husband and father, it was important to try and make a future for my family. So in April 2006, I started working as a security guard for the government in Ramallah, another part of Palestine near Rafah. It wasn't an easy job to do but there were not many jobs around at the time so I was grateful to get this one. I was posted at the border between Egypt and Gaza. My mission: to stop prohibited goods like drugs and weapons coming into Gaza. Every day we stopped many people trying to smuggle in all kinds of things like guns and grenades. But no matter how hard they tried, we were pretty thorough and I am sure we did a good job keeping Gaza safe. It was tough but satisfying work, so the first few months passed quickly.

On a hot August night a few months later, I was sitting on a small stone rock wall outside my home in Rafah because, once again, our camp had no electricity. Power cuts became frequent after the Hamas, an Islamic Terrorist Group, seized Gaza. I guess we just all had to get used to it. I was sitting on the wall watching people cruise by when I received a telephone call from someone I hadn't heard from for a while.

"Hi, Raed, how are you?"

"Hi, Ismail! I'm good, thanks. What about you?"

"I'm good too. Hey, are you busy?"

"No. Why what's wrong?"

"Nothing, I just want to visit you."

"Of course, that would be great," I sighed with relief, knowing that my best friend was safe in our deadly and dangerous strip.

"OK, then, I'll be there shortly."

"Great, see you soon."

I felt really happy that Ismail was coming to see me. Not only was Ismail my closest friend, we both had been so busy working that we hadn't seen each other for a long time. Within half an hour Ismail arrived and sat next to me on the stone wall. We chatted about our day and planned a visit to the beach later that night. The weather was so hot and sticky at this time of year that the idea of cooling ourselves with a swim at the beach sounded nice.

All of a sudden, the muggy night was interrupted by the sound of angry shouting and people fighting down the street. Upon hearing the commotion nearby, Ismail and I stood up and headed towards the noise. When we arrived at a house down the street, I saw the figure of a man in an upstairs window. I scrutinised the man's face carefully. Almost instantly, I realised who it was. A man called Nedal, who worked for a military wing of the Hamas Terrorist Group. When I looked at him more closely, I noticed he was holding in his hand a long, metal object. I recognised it to be an Automatic Kalashnikov 47 machine gun. I watched Nedal slowly raise his rifle to the window and aim it at a man in the street below. I knew that man – it was Ramzy. Ramzy once worked for a government that was overtaken by the Hamas party. This automatically made Ramzy an "enemy" of the Hamas. I watched Nedal pointing his gun at Ramzy. "Rat-a-ta-tat!!" Nedal had squeezed the trigger. Within a fraction of a second, Ramzy was lying on the ground.

The front door of Nedal's house flew wide open. Nedal marched over to Ramzy's motionless body for a quick look and then he swung himself around and hurried down the street as if nothing had happened. I could not believe Nedal's brutal behaviour. "Hey! Why did you shoot him?!"

My question stopped Nedal dead in his tracks. He turned towards me slowly and hissed with hot, acid burning in his voice:

"If you don't be quiet, *you* will be next!"

Then, without even heeding his own warning, Nedal raised his AK-47 again. This time he wasn't aiming at Ramzy, he was aiming directly at *me*. At that moment, time warped. In a slow motion kind of way, I watched Nedal pull the trigger of his gun. The pain was instant and excruciating. I felt as if a fire had been lit inside my body. I was burning alive on the spot. Nedal had shot me! When the speeding bullet entered my upper left arm, it blasted the bone and muscle and exited through the other side. Once the bullet left my shattered arm, it kept going. I heard it strike something behind me. I turned around to see where the bullet had landed. Oh no! It had hit Ismail. He was lying on the ground, curled up in a weird way, not moving. I saw that the bullet had pierced Ismail's abdomen, causing his stomach to burst open. There was blood everywhere and his organs started falling out. I was in so much pain after the bullet tore up my arm that I couldn't do anything. I didn't even realise what was actually happening.

After hearing gunfire in the street, my family rushed out of the house. Immediately, they ran towards us. All they saw was blood spurting out of my arm, and blood and guts everywhere. My uncle placed his hand on my arm where I had been shot to slow the blood flow down. My brother Ayman kneeled down on the ground and lifted Ismail into his arms. Then Ayman started walking down the street to find a taxi to take Ismail to hospital. Ismail was in a bad state and a taxi would get him there more quickly than waiting for an ambulance. It was Friday in Gaza, a Holy day, a holiday, so public transport in Palestine was scarce. After stopping a taxi, my brother loaded Ismail into the car and they took off to the hospital. In the meantime, our street filled with people who ventured out of their homes to see what had happened. Eventually, an ambulance arrived and took me to hospital too.

The next thing I remember was arriving at the hospital and being taken to an examination room. A doctor examined me there, administered first aid, and then ordered X-rays. While I was lying on the bed in pain waiting for the doctor to return, Ismail's older brother Mohammad Koshtar came over. His face was white and his expression blank.

"Hello, Raed."

"Hello, Mohammad."

"Are you all right?"

"I don't know – my arm – pain – burning – hurts," I stuttered.

"Raed, I need to ask you something," Mohammad was solemn. "Who shot my brother?"

"Nedal," I replied quietly, miserably, still in a state of shock myself.

"Sorry – could not stop – very fast."

Then Mohammad just left. He looked terrible, and very upset.

By this time, many members of Ismail's family had gathered together at the hospital. Some people who saw me talking with Mohammad approached me to say: "What did Mohammad just ask you?" I gave everyone the same reply: "Nedal did it. Nedal shot Ismail." When the hospital finished X-raying me and the doctor bandaged up my arm securely, I was transferred to another hospital. When I arrived there, I was surprised. Ramzy, the man who Nedal first shot, was resting comfortably in bed. His whole family was at his side. Fortunately, Ramzy wasn't fatally wounded at all. The bullets struck his leg, causing minor injuries.

My friend Ismail was not so lucky. Ismail did not have the luxury of resting in a hospital bed like Ramzy. He was not receiving medical care to treat his wound. He was not being spoiled with hugs and kisses from family. For Ismail, it was the worst possible scenario. He was lying on a cold, steel tray in the morgue, alone. Poor Ismail, my best friend, was dead. After that, I remained hospitalised for a while. I am not sure how long exactly. I had nothing to do there except think about my murdered friend.

Soon afterwards, the doctor visited me.

"Mr Zanoon, how are you today?"

"Hello, doctor, not bad. How are you?"

"Very good, thank you. Well, your arm is fine and I will be discharging you from hospital later today. There will be no need for an operation," he said.

"Really? Are you sure?" I asked apprehensively.

"Yes, your arm is fine," the doctor replied.

A feeling of anxiety registered deeply in my mind. Something definitely *wasn't* right. *If my arm was as good as the doctor claimed, then why was I still in so much pain?* My father arrived to pick me up from hospital soon after. We caught a local taxi and headed home. It was good to be back. I missed my family so much during my hospital stay. Once I arrived home, I was inundated with visitors. Everyone came to see how I was. It was nice. One visitor informed me that the man who shot Ramzy, me and Ismail was just seen praying inside the local Mosque. What?! A cold-blooded killer *praying*? That's sick! I heard later that many people in our neighbourhood were very angry that Nedal shot up our street. They wanted to take revenge on him. But they never got their chance. Shortly after the shooting, the police arrested Nedal for his crime and put him in jail.

It is a pleasant August morning a few days later when my mother wakes me gently from my sleep. I open my eyes to see my mum's hand resting upon my good shoulder. Then I notice a sad look upon my mum's face. She looks as if she is about to cry, there is so much sorrow in her eyes.

"Raed, Raed, wake up, son," she says softly.

"Good morning, Mum."

"Good morning, son," she says, trying to smile.

"It is Ismail's funeral today... "

"NOOOOOOOOOOOOOO!"

All of a sudden, I go into shock. Everything becomes surreal. Memories and reality blur.

"NOOOOOOOOOO!" Ismail can't be dead! We are going for a swim together at the beach!

Then the flashback hits me. I see Nedal standing before me with his AK-47. I hear the gunshot. I smell smoke, powder, blood, and death. Startled, I sit up in my bed. Tears start streaming down my face. I cannot believe it. Ismail, my best friend, is dead.

"But he can't be dead, I only spoke to him the other day," my mind insists.

"Raed," a soft voice interrupts my gruesome flashback.

"Ismail isn't coming back, he is dead. Today is his funeral, Raed, I am sorry," my mum says.

I cannot believe what is happening. I rise to my feet, wash and dress, and go outside to wait with my father. Although my dad says nothing, I sense that he was very worried about me because of what happened to Ismail. Ismail and I were the best of friends and we would do anything to help one another. When I get out of my mind and look around the yard outside, I notice people standing around looking very sad and some of them are crying. My mind doesn't want me to believe Ismail is gone. How could he be? I was just speaking to him on the phone.

My family and I visit Ismail's home to pay our respects to Ismail and his family. We sit there and wait for Ismail's body to arrive from the morgue. Finally Ismail, poor Ismail, comes home. I try to bid him farewell properly, but it is impossible to get anywhere near him. So many other people are trying to say goodbye to him too. I just wanted to scream at everyone to: "Get away from my friend!" I just wanted to be close to him one last time. My grief is intolerable; it boils inside, burning me. I desperately need fresh air so I storm out of the house, and hide behind a neighbour's fence. Falling to the ground on my knees and crying inconsolably, I vomit. I am devastated, sick, broken. I have lost my best friend forever.

After ten terrible minutes I still feel sick but it is time to take Ismail's body to the local Mosque. We all walk down the street together – a little funeral procession to the Mosque. We go inside, kneel down on the floor, and pray for Ismail. "Please let Ismail arrive safely to Heaven," I pray. After the prayers finish we approach Ismail's body. Except for his face, he is wrapped neatly in clean, white sheets. It looks like he is sleeping. "Please, God, take care of Ismail, he is a wonderful man and deserves the best in Heaven. I know he will get all that he needs and wants when he is beside you." Then my grief and guilt rear up like a wounded bull inside my heart: "I am so sorry I wasn't there to help you, Ismail!" I suddenly scream and cry. "We have been friends for so long that you are more like a brother to me... Please forgive me, Ismail. One day we will be together in Heaven. I will miss you so much." After saying goodbye to Ismail, I hover gently over Ismail and watch his body being taken to the Rafah Cemetery where he is finally laid to rest. Ismail was only 18 years old when he died. He had not done the things he wanted to do in life. He was far too young to die. My arm aches so much that it wakes me up abruptly, disturbing my dream about death and funerals. My mouth is forced open and yellow vomit gushes out all over my clean hospital gown.

Two months pass and my arm gets worse. It develops a rancid smell and the pain is stronger than ever. My mother thought it was gangrene so we have to act quickly. My father travels to Gaza City to look for a private doctor. "Don't worry, Raed. Everything will be fine, son," my mum gently reassures me, stroking my sweaty brow. A few hours later, my father returns home. He has found a private doctor in Gaza willing to help us. The next morning my parents and I go to see the doctor. Upon arriving, the doctor examines my arm and immediately orders X-rays. When the urgent X-ray results come back later that day, the doctor studies them carefully and then he turns to me with a serious look on his face. "Raed, you need a major operation to fix your arm," he reports gravely. "The surgery is risky. To survive it, you must have a matching blood donor."

I try to make sense of this news, which was both good and bad. At least the private doctor confirmed my gut feeling. I have always felt that there was something wrong with my arm, long after the first hospital doctor told me that I didn't need an operation. The bad news was that there is a high risk I could lose my arm, or worse, lose my life if I couldn't find a matching blood donor soon. After receiving the private doctor's medical advice, we return home. I try not to worry too much about my arm. However, my arm and the surgery is all I can think about.

Later that night a cousin named Majid Zanoon drops in to see me. Even though I am happy to see him and try to chat cheerfully, I cannot stop worrying about my arm. My bright cousin senses this. "What's wrong, cousin?" Majid asks. I tell Majid all about my visit to the private doctor, what he said about the surgery, and the need for a blood donor. Unexpectedly, Majid smiles.

"If possible, I would like to be your blood donor, Raed," Majid declares earnestly.

"What?! Are you sure?"

"Yep, it would be an honour," he confirms.

"I don't know what to say, this means so much to me," I exclaim.

The next day the private doctor checks our blood. The results couldn't be better. Majid is a compatible donor. I am excited and relieved. But at the same time, I start to feel sick, really sick. By this time, the state of my arm is so bad that if I want to save it, or my life, there is no more time to lose. That day I am booked to have surgery in a local Gaza hospital where the private doctor is waiting for me ready to operate. The nurses dress me in a long white gown, place me in a bed, and prepare me for my long operation. I don't remember at all what happened after that. The anaesthetic must have knocked me out.

I heard that my surgery lasted over twelve hours. Apparently, the surgeons inserted a metal plate into my arm and secured it into place using eight screws. It was a very long procedure but an essential one to save my arm. Nedal's bullet had destroyed the bone completely and badly damaged the surrounding muscle and flesh. I also understand that my father Abdul Hakim Zanoon – the really angry one who smashed the house to pieces and threw pots and pans at my head – sat outside the operating room for the whole duration of my surgery with the patience of an angel.

When I wake up after surgery, the first thing I see when I open my eyes is my father Abdul Hakim. He is sitting on a chair in the hospital corridor just outside my room. I notice he is holding his head in his hands. When he looks up at me, I see tears running down his face. Then he gets up, approaches my bed, puts his arms around me, and gives me a big hug. I look up at him and smile.

"Dad?"

"Yes, son?"

"How long was my operation?"

"Over twelve hours, Raed," he says looking earnestly into my eyes.

"Is everything all right?" I ask.

"Yes, son. I talked to the doctor and everything is fine. You should make a full recovery."

I smile at my dad and close my eyes. At last, the ordeal regarding my arm is over, I think to myself. I have survived another day inside the Gaza Strip of death.

After several days in hospital recovering from surgery, I am discharged, given medication, and returned back home. But my peaceful rest doesn't last long. I am *still* in intense pain. Why? I thought that once I had this operation my arm would be good. But I am wrong, very wrong. The searing pain continues and does not go away at all. Not even five months later, by which time Nedal, the man who gunned three people down in our street, is released from prison. I start to feel very afraid every time I think about Nedal and his AK-47 because who knows what he is going to do next. My fear is not unfounded. I soon find out I am right to trust my instinct.

One day, when I am feeling brave enough, I venture out into the street. Bad luck! I bump into Nedal straight away! He stares at me with a furious look on his face and it is clear he cannot contain his rage. "Remember when I killed your friend?" he yells at me across the street, his voice bubbling over with strong, corrosive acid. "Well, now I am going to kill *you*!!!"

In a flurry of fear and panic, I turn around and run back home as fast as I can. I lock all the doors and shut up all the windows. After bumping into Nedal, I don't dare leave the house again that day. In fact, I refuse to leave the house for weeks. I feel safer at home. A long time passes by until I finally find the courage to go outside again. It is hard to go outside for many reasons. I am still in great pain and I cannot use my arm. My best friend was shot dead. A Hamas guerrilla made a death threat against me. And the horror of being murdered at any time is too frightening. From then on, every day and every night, all day and all night, I live in fear of my life. Although the constant physical pain in my arm is excruciating, the mental pain is much worse. My strongest fears keep me hyper vigilant all day, and wide awake all night. And when I finally do sleep, the terrifying nightmares wake me up and disturb my rest. *"I cannot live like this!"* I scream in my mind. I am living in a Gaza Hell!

Despite all my fear, nightmares, flashbacks, and more – I force myself to take healthy action. "Come on, Raed! Get out of bed, eat something, do something," I start telling myself every day. "You can't hide away for the rest of your life." I try to be positive. I have to be – or else the hopelessness corrodes my soul. Eventually, one morning several months after Nedal threatens to kill me, I make myself step beyond the front door of my house and walk into the street outside. I look up at the clear blue sky.

Somehow, I convince myself to savour this brief moment of pleasure. For the first time in ages, it feels good to be outside after staying indoors for so long. It feels good to let the sun shine on my face.

Gaza Burning (2007–2009)

Yea, thou [sic] I walk through the valley of the shadow of death,
I will fear no evil; for thou art with me;
Thy rod and thy staff, they comfort me.
Thou preparest a table before me
In the presence of mine enemies.
– Psalms (23:4–5)

In Gaza, tension between the Fatah Government and the Hamas Terrorist Group grew. It became so great that the Hamas established their own government and parliament. That year the government I was working for sadly lost the parliamentary election. This resulted in the Hamas taking over Gaza. Once they took control of everything in Gaza they got rid of all the officials from the previous government. This also divided the people of Palestine who were now ruled by two opposing governments: Fatah and Hamas. A tragic outcome at this time was that over seven hundred people were shot and killed by Hamas Terrorists. In one particularly cruel and brazen act of terror, Hamas soldiers pushed over one hundred and fifty innocent people from rooftops and buildings. Many people who protested against the Hamas were killed or injured during the violent riots at this time. The conflict between the two groups became so volatile and dangerous that life became impossible in Gaza. The Hamas Terrorist Organization attacked my old work locations on a daily basis and constantly fired rockets at the Fatah Palestinian Army. As such, it was not safe to work in Gaza at all anymore. Everyone was advised to stay indoors. Due to the ongoing nature of deadly Hamas terrorist activities, people like me who had been working for the Fatah Army (an oppositional government) had to stay at home. However, the Fatah continued paying our salaries. I was grateful to receive some regular income, especially with a family to support and two children of my own to clothe and feed. Staying at home also meant I could spend more time with my sons and family – and I was very happy about that. But the salary was small and the money not enough. Life was hard. At times, we did not have any food to eat at all.

Soon all the surrounding borders around Gaza were closed off and a blockade was imposed on all of us. There were more power cuts and no petrol at all for cars or motorbikes. Many people started to run their vehicles on cooking oil. Life was getting worse, more like a graveyard of living humans, more and more like hell. There was much poverty now and unemployment was widespread. Many of the local businesses were forced to shut down. This increased unemployment levels even more, while access to basic necessities decreased. Much worse, something terrible happened during this time. We learnt that the Hamas in Gaza had performed a malicious feat. They crept into Egypt inside the smuggling tunnels near my home and kidnapped an Israeli soldier named Gilad Shalit in an underground raid. The soldier was held captive in a secret location for more than five years. No one knew of his whereabouts, not even if he was dead or alive. As a result of this kidnapping, Israel declared war on Gaza.

At the same time, my family life was at the height of a war zone too. I had already spent two years living apart from my wife Asma because I could not stand her constantly arguing and spitting at me. Now she was mistreating our children. She became very self-absorbed and only gave her attention to our first-born son, Jehad. She totally ignored our second son, Rayan. In fact, she never gave Rayan any affection or positive attention at all. All he wanted was a smile or a hug – the love of a caring mother. However, Asma just yelled at him and pushed him aside as if he was a piece of garbage. One morning after waking up and watching Asma mistreat my son, I showered, dressed, and marched straight to the courthouse to file for a divorce. Enough was enough. I could not stand Asma's Hamas-like cruelty towards the children anymore. The divorce process was finalised after a few months. Asma took the dowry money but left the children behind. So I took custody of my two sons, who have lived with my parents and siblings ever since. Although my family is poor, my two little boys have always received lots of affection from their grandparents, aunts, uncles and cousins. At least the war at home was over.

The conflict in Gaza worsened over time. On the 27th of December 2008, Israel attacked Gaza. The aim of this war was to stop all the rocket fire that was (and still is) originating from Gaza to Israel. It also sought to stop all the weapon smuggling going on inside the tunnels underneath Gaza. At this time, I remember Palestinian groups firing many rockets from Gaza. A ground invasion of Gaza commenced on the 3rd of January 2009. So while the rest of the world was partying to welcome in the New Year, we were hiding and fighting for our lives. Everyone who lived in the Rafah Compound could hear the rumbling of the tanks as they approached. The sound of rockets whizzed so loudly past my windows every day it was deafening. Sometimes, when rockets flew very close by, the doors, windows, and dishes shook so badly that the glass shattered. On many occasions, I was too afraid to breathe, just in case the Israeli forces heard me and shot me. The war, named "Operation Cast Lead" lasted three whole weeks.

During this war, over a thousand Palestinians lost their lives at the hands of Israeli forces. Most of the deaths were young children and babies. At this time, I saw many people die. All the while, I was trying to raise my sons and help the rest of my family to survive by hiding from the onslaught. As a local, I know that terrible military mistakes were made. Although Israel targeted offices they believed to be occupied by Hamas Terrorists, many times the missiles missed their targets, hitting the homes of innocent Palestinians instead. The whole war was futile and pointless because all the important Hamas officials were hiding underneath the Mosques in trenches and beneath hospitals where they thought they would be safe. The Hamas hid themselves away like cowards, leaving innocent Palestinian people to suffer and die in their places. Who will stop firing rockets first, Gaza or Israel? No one wants to stop. As such, the Hamas and Fatah keep on arguing in noisy, crowded streets, over the bodies of their dead loved ones.

Because of war, I remember we had so little of everything in Gaza. Gas, drinking water, and food were scarce. Times were harder than ever, much harder than anything before. Where could people possibly find the funds to rebuild their homes and their lives after everything was taken away from them? Even if you did have the money and materials to build your home, this was impractical – impossible. This is because of restrictions and blockades Israel imposed on us. As a result, a basic building supply like cement was hard to get. We had to rely on global charities to help with food and other necessities. Gaza continued to receive donations from the global community to ease our pain and suffering. As usual, however, every time any goods entered Gaza the government grabbed it all. No matter what was sent to us, we civilians received nothing. It seemed that our government loved to see us all suffer and starve. Medicines sent to help those wounded from the war were sold to rich buyers. This caused many badly wounded people to die. Even food sent to us in Gaza ended up in the hands of the Hamas Government. The Hamas even sold the food to purchase more weapons so they could continue fighting Israel. Nothing was given to poor civilians. We Palestinians received nothing at all.

One night I tried to leave my hiding place to look for food. My family and my sons were extremely hungry because we hadn't eaten for three weeks. The main priority was to survive, and by now, we were starving. When I left my secret hiding spot, I saw to my horror the Hamas forces standing near me in the street. As soon as they spotted me they stared long and hard at me with weapons in their hands. They probably thought I was working for Israel. But I wasn't. I was just trying to find some food for my family. I felt so afraid when I saw them that I immediately went back home. I didn't go anywhere near them. We went without food for another night.

At long last, about a year later on the 18th of January 2010, a ceasefire was announced. But this was not really true. In reality, the war continued because I could still hear the sounds of rockets in the sky above us. When we all left our hiding places the first thing I noticed was all the mass destruction around us. Many houses were completely destroyed. All that was left of the many houses just down the road from us was a huge pile of rubble and debris. I went with my family to see if our home was still there. We were overjoyed to find it actually still standing – even though all the doors and windows were gone. We went inside to have a look at the extent of the damage. We noticed that many of the interior walls were damaged. Still, we were the lucky ones.

After the Gaza War was over, I tried to establish a normal routine in abnormal conditions. We scavenged the neighbourhood for food. But we were feeling so depressed and hopeless, we knew we needed to nourish ourselves spiritually as well as physically. I started attending prayers at the local Mosque every Friday with my family. One Friday, the Hamas Terrorists were there. The Imam (Muslim priest) was talking about death and killing people in the name of Islam and saying things like: "Kill the Israelis! Kill the Americans! Kill all non-Muslims!" I was shocked. Not once did he talk about anything spiritually uplifting or refer to lovely passages from the Quran. All of a sudden, a voice from the back of the Mosque shouted out in defiance: "We are here to learn about Islam and peace! Not about the Hamas and the killing of innocent people! All we want to do is pray to Allah, our GOD!"

An uproar swept through the Mosque in an instant. A throng

of angry faces turned in the direction of the outspoken voice that had dared to interrupt the violent political speech. I thought I recognised the voice of this outspoken man so I turned around to see who had shouted. It was my Uncle Abdel-Latif! He was the rebellious one! After this incident, our family left the Mosque immediately. We decided we would no longer attend the Mosque for prayers. From now on, we would pray at home. That way, we wouldn't have to listen to Islamic terrorists talk about killing people.

That same day, after leaving the Mosque, we all went the house of my Uncle Abdel-Latif. After eating a delicious lunch of magloba (Arabic chicken and rice) and drinking some Coca Cola as a treat, we decided to sit outside his house in the fresh air and chat. My uncle's son, Kamal Zanoon, was sitting quietly in the street when suddenly he fixed his gaze into the distance. Three black vehicles were approaching us. As the cars got closer to my uncle's house, we noticed that each vehicle contained at least ten passengers all dressed in black. Their faces were completely covered by black balaclavas and they were wielding weapons. Oh no! They are Hamas rebels! We all bolted inside my uncle's house as fast as our legs could carry us, except for my cousin Kamal. For some reason, Kamal just stood in the street and stared. I headed upstairs to a room above the street and opened the window to get a better view of what was happening below. The three black Jeeps cruised slowly past my uncle's house. "BANG!" A loud gunshot tore open the silence of our Holy Day. A Hamas rebel just shot Kamal. My cousin fell to the ground in pain. Without a doubt, this was an attempt by the Hamas to retaliate against my uncle who spoke up earlier at the Mosque.

Many people in the surrounding houses heard the gunshots so they went outside to see what was happening. Once they realised that the Hamas officials shot my cousin Kamal, they armed themselves with bricks, rocks, large stones, and anything they could lay their hands on. They used whatever objects they could pick up – throwing things and launching everything at the Hamas and their cars with all their might. The Hamas Terrorists retaliated back with full force. They began shooting up the sky with a storm of bullets, trying to disperse the local crowd that had gathered there to support Kamal and his dad.

The Zanoon family members who lived close by went home and headed to their rooftops where they too started throwing bricks down at the Hamas and their cars. Dints on bonnets and broken car windows made the sleek Hamas vehicles look ugly. I loved it! Eventually the Hamas left! Hooray! We cheered! We felt victorious and happy! But not for long. Moments later the Hamas returned. This time they brought with them more Hamas rebels. That's when we all realised that these terrorists hadn't left at all but had in fact gone to get extra military reinforcement. Rocks against machine guns – it was not even a fair fight! The Hamas started firing bullets into our homes. Soldiers broke into Uncle Abdel-Latif's house, arresting him and Kamal (who was still writhing in the street after being shot in his legs). Both of them were dragged savagely away to prison. It was a scene from a horror movie, except that it was really happening.

Two days later, my Uncle Abdel-Latif and my cousin Kamal were released from prison and returned back home. Only then was Kamal admitted to hospital to receive medical attention for the gunshot wounds to his legs. Our uncle told us about his terrifying experience in prison. The Hamas soldiers beat his face and body for two days. He had no food, no water, no light, no sleep, and no peace the whole time. After that, I hardly ever left my house. I thought it was safer to stay indoors away from the outside world. Maybe for weeks or maybe months, I sat around the house biding time. I watched television, raised my two sons, and played card games to give my mind a rest from worry, a break from my mental pain.

Palestine "Peace Dove"

The wings of hope carry us, soaring high above the driving winds of life.
– Anna Jacob

Milk Magic

A really good thing about the Rafah Refugee Camp in Gaza where I lived is that it had schools. The bad thing was that it was very hard for children to study well at school. After all, we would often be kept awake all night by the sound of bomb raids and gunfire. This made it extremely hard for children like me to concentrate on schoolwork. Tired and unsettled, many children would find it difficult to be happy or to make good friends. It was easy for children to fall behind in their studies quickly. This made some teachers very, very angry. In fact, some teachers were so angry that they would hit and beat the children. I guess the teachers thought that if they did that it would make the children learn more quickly and effectively. But it didn't. It just made things worse.

Since many people in Gaza are not well educated due to all the displacement, violence, and war there, how can parents possibly help their children to get ahead in school? So children become depressed and hopeless early in life, well before their lives even have a chance to begin. Tired, hungry, failing their studies, beaten by teachers, it doesn't take long for children to start hating school. I myself noticed that children looked happier playing outside because their minds were focussed on play, I guess – not on tough teachers, hard lessons, and the misery of school life. Every day after school, I saw children go outside into the dirty streets to play because there was nothing else for them to do. In Gaza, we have no shopping malls, game arcades, parks or playgrounds. In fact, no one has anything at all. All the children have to play with is the dirt and the dust on the ground outside their homes and whatever rocks, rubbish and scraps they can find to occupy themselves.

Since most parents couldn't afford to give children pocket money to buy food at school, most children were hungry at school all day. One day I was walking past a school near my house and noticed something that weighed heavily on my heart. I saw a young boy standing alone in the schoolyard. A group of students next to him were eating sweets, crisps and other treats that they just bought with their pocket money. I saw his eyes follow their hands as they brought the delicious snacks up to their mouths. The little boy just stood in the schoolyard and watched the others eat their food. It was clear that he didn't have any pocket money to buy anything from the snack cart. I felt sad that everyone was eating, and that this hungry child was not. All the other children were just eating their food as if they had no cares in the world at all and this one little boy just stood there, alone, a look of longing on his sad face. I would have loved to see that boy get just a little taste of food but it was clear that the other children weren't going to share. Although it was awful to watch, it made me wonder and ask myself: "What I can I do?" My subconscious mind must have heard me. Not long afterwards, I thought of a brilliant idea.

A few months after watching the hungry boy at school, I worked very hard and saved up nearly US$100. With this money to spare in my pocket, I was rich. I went into the local store to see what they had. I decided to buy some milk. In fact, I bought around five hundred cartons. I bought so much milk that I had to ask some friends to help me carry it from the shop. We walked around the corner to a place I know children like to play. We stacked all the milk cartons on the ground and headed over to where the children were playing. "Hey! Who wants free milk?" Well, as soon as the children heard me say that, they all rushed over to the huge stack of milk cartons. They looked so happy and their faces beamed brightly. I handed each child a carton of milk and they happily drank it. As soon as these children finished drinking their milk, more children arrived. Children from the neighbouring refugee camps had heard about the free milk too. In fact, children came from everywhere. Goodness gracious! I felt like a sorcerer luring children out their hiding places with the magic of milk. I was overwhelmed, but delighted. I had never seen so many children gather together in the same place before. Somehow the news about a nice "milk man" giving away free milk had spread through the strip faster than a frown spreads on the face of an angry Hamas soldier. All the children were shouting: "Can I have a carton of milk?" and "Please, Uncle, can I have some?" I was inundated. For the next hour or so children came and went to collect their milk and then leave. I noticed that some children came back for a second helping. I didn't have the heart to say, "No, you've just had some milk," so I handed out more cartons to them. When the last few children left and all the milk was gone, I felt content inside. The children didn't drink much milk in Gaza because it was so expensive. So it felt fantastic to be able to give them some. Seeing the huge smiles on the children's faces and the white moustaches around their mouths was all worth it.

School Mission

Another time I had some money left over after buying food for my family. I remember sitting outside that day watching kids playing in the street. I noticed that many of the children didn't have any footwear on their feet. This made me feel sad. The Rafah Compound where I lived had hundreds of extremely poor families. These families were so poor that they could not even manage to buy their children anything for school. I hated the idea of young children starting their new school year with no school supplies at all and nothing to boost their self-esteem. Therefore, I decided to visit a store in Rafah that sells bags. There, I bought about 100 backpacks. This felt so good that I wandered over to another store in Rafah that sells stationery. I purchased pencils, erasers, sharpeners and rulers. With happiness in my heart and help from a couple of friends, I gathered all the school supplies and headed home. I asked my family to help me fill each bag with stationery. We placed one item of each type of stationery in every backpack for children in our neighbourhood. I was ready to launch my 'school mission'.

My family and I visited the homes of the poorest families in Rafah. We asked the parents if they would like their children to have a little 'back to school' gift. Of course, all the parents were overjoyed about the idea that their children would get goodies for school. As for the children, they were hilarious. You see, our back to school mission involved putting a bag on the back of each child. But as soon as I would finish sliding bags on the children's backs, off the bags came! At first, I thought that the children didn't like their new bags. However, when I realised what they were doing, I cracked up with laughter. The children were so excited about getting their school gifts, that they couldn't resist taking their packs off and looking inside. They immediately sat down on the floor next to each other and opened up the zips of the bags. After peering inside their bags, they took out *all* the items. They were so surprised to see pretty stationery inside their schoolbags. All the children inspected their merchandise carefully before putting the items back inside their bags. After that, every single child's face beamed. To see the children so happy with big smiles on their faces definitely made my miserable life in Gaza happier, even if it was only for a while.

Frontline Rescue

One night in 2002 just after midnight, I was woken up by the sound of helicopters whirring loudly in the sky above. Shortly afterwards I heard gunshots and bombs dropping everywhere. I climbed out of bed and raced downstairs to be with my family.

We all went outside knowing instinctively that we had to move to a safe place. As our home was right next to the border of Egypt, this made it one of the most dangerous places to be. I looked at my brother Ayman.

"What's happening now?" I asked.

"It's another invasion, Raed."

We left our home out of danger's way and headed over to the safety of my sister's home. A few seconds after arriving there, I heard a missile fly right by us and explode in the very next street. It had just been fired by the helicopter above. I ran over to the next street as fast as I could. When I arrived there, all I could see was billowing clouds of dust and smoke. As the dust began to settle, I heard somebody shouting:

"Help me! Help me!"

I shouted to some people to call for an ambulance, and approached a man lying in the street who looked as if he was the one shouting. I put my arms around him and hugged him. It was clear he was badly hurt.

"What's your name?"

"I am Khalid Hammad."

"My name is Raed."

"Please, Raed, help me," begged Khalid.

I continued to hug Khalid until the ambulance arrived. Once the paramedics attended the scene, I left Khalid in their care. I scoured the place to see if anyone else nearby needed any help. I found another wounded man lying in a fresh pile of rubble and I tried desperately to help him. Unfortunately, I was too late. By the time the paramedics came to him he had already passed away. I felt so sad and guilty that he died. In fact, many people were killed that day. I wish I could have helped everyone so that they didn't have to lose their lives. The guilt I felt was unbearable.

I remember another time in 2002, it was about 4 o'clock in the afternoon and I was at home sleeping. I was woken up by the sound of bombs firing from a nearby tank. Many loud explosions were occurring in rapid succession, one straight after the other. The bombing continued all night, and I remember lying in my bed feeling really scared. The next day I awoke with a huge fright. The house was shaking terribly, as were all the doors and windows. I was so scared that I ran outside. The street was full of frightened people – men, women and children. They were crying, crouching and trying to hide. They all seemed to have come from the border of Egypt and Palestine. I looked up at the sky and noticed it was filled with thick, black smoke from a massive explosion. Instinctively, I dashed across to where the explosions had occurred. At the time, I did not even realise I was barefoot. The only thing that was going through my mind was that I needed to see what had happened. I needed to help as many people as I could. As I was passing by a small room with the door open in the Rafah Refugee Compound, I noticed many people in there crying, screaming and shouting. My friend Mohi was with them.

"Mohi, what happened?" I asked.

"The Israeli tanks have bombed Gaza and many people have been killed," he replied.

I looked around and saw that one of the recent explosions had just hit a local minimarket near our home. The force of the explosion was so strong that it completely destroyed the store. It was owned and managed by a nice man who had a wife and family. I called Mohi over so we could get a better look and we noticed that the front of the store was completely barricaded in with big chunks of concrete and building debris. We went around to the manager's home behind the minimarket and made a hole in the wall large enough for Mohi and me to climb through. We both climbed into the store and found some members of the manager's family there. We helped them to leave the danger of their collapsing home through the hole we made. Once we escorted the manager's family to a safe place, Mohi and I returned to the minimarket to see if any other people were trapped inside. We entered the hole and started looking around for survivors. When we came to a large fridge in the shop, I noticed that its door was wide open. I glanced behind the door on to the floor and noticed the body of a man lying there in a big pool of blood – it was the manager. I peered around the door to get a better look. I thought I was going to collapse from the huge shock of what I saw there. It was only half a man – the manager's legs had been blown off completely by shrapnel and they were severed from his hips.

We found it very hard to help this poor man or even move what was left of him because of the terrible state of his body. It was also hard to get to him because the fridge was in the way and it was too heavy for us to shift. But the man was a human being – our store manager, my neighbour – and I didn't want to give up and just leave him there all alone. We went outside again and found something that looked like a large metal rod or skewer. We inserted the skewer into a broken window from outside, slid it underneath the manager's clothes, and started to pull his body out of the store. We laid the store manager gently in the street. After that, we went back into the store and looked everywhere to make sure that there was no one else left in there. Hidden behind the fridge we noticed the body of another man. We were able to carry him outside into the street where other people started helping us. Finding the manager's family and pulling people out of the minimarket made Mohi and I very tired. When we finished we both headed back to our homes.

I was so upset about everything that happened that I decided not to return to my parents' home because I would be alone there. I decided to visit my grandfather's home instead. My aunties and uncles were there and all of them were sitting on the floor crying.

"What's wrong?" I asked. I thought it was the shock and terror of the Israeli attack itself that had upset them so much.

"Tonight's bombing has killed your cousin!" they all cried. "Shaima Kamal Abu Shamala is dead!" I froze. My beautiful cousin Shaima was still a baby. She was just nine years old. My relatives told me that a large piece of shrapnel from the strong explosion pierced her head. It killed her instantly. I didn't know what to say, or feel, or think. It was a total massacre that day, and as a result, many innocent people, including my little cousin, lost their lives.

When I looked around at my relatives who all lived in the same area as the minimarket manager, they were crying inconsolably. It was not long before I too started crying for the death of my cousin. Then one of my aunties looked up at me and noticed the way I looked. "Raed?! What happened to you? Are you OK?"

I inspected myself and noticed that my clothes were completely soaked in blood.

"Yes, I'm fine," I sobbed. "I helped some wounded people after the explosion."

Then I spotted my father sitting there amongst his grieving brothers and sisters. He looked visibly upset.

"Raed, it was very brave of you to help those people. But can you please go home and have a shower? You are completely covered in blood, and you look and smell awful," he said solemnly.

I nodded to him and headed for the door.

Just before I could slip through the doorway, I felt something warm grab my hand. It was my mother. She looked deeply and tenderly into my eyes, leaned over to the side of my face, and whispered in my ear: "I am so proud of you, son. You are a true Palestinian 'peace dove' and I love you with all my heart." Then my mum kissed me on the cheek and let me go. To this day, my mum's message remains one of the most beautiful and unforgettable moments of my life.

I don't know how long I showered for that night because I just kept thinking about what had happened. My dead cousin, people lying in the street, the store manager with no legs, my mother's lovely message. The shock of witnessing half a body must have kicked in because straight after I finished my shower, I threw up. After washing my face and rinsing my mouth, I changed into some clean clothes and wandered back over to my grandfather's home. Shortly after arriving there, everyone started to leave. I followed the silent procession to see where they were going. They were heading for the local hospital to see my cousin Shaima. Everyone was in an acute state of grief and kept crying relentlessly. When we arrived at the morgue, I looked over at my Aunt Raam Hussein, Shaima's mother. I noticed she was talking quietly to her dead daughter:

"Why did you leave me, Shaima?" my auntie asked, over and over.

After asking Shaima this repeatedly, my auntie started to scream and punch herself in the face. I didn't know what to do. I walked over to my auntie, placed my arm gently around her shoulders, and gave her a light hug. I took a bottle of water from her hand, poured a small amount into the palm of my hand, and gently dabbed my auntie's face. I was so relieved when this soothed her a little. A short while after this, we had to leave the morgue.

The very next morning Shaima was transferred from the hospital morgue to the local Mosque. Our family went to Shaima's funeral to pray for her safe arrival to Heaven. Under gloomy skies and with heavy hearts, we watched Shaima's tiny little body get buried in the cold dirt inside the lonely graveyard at the back of Rafah. I wondered and worried what would become of Shaima's soul. Surely, the constant sound of fighting near the Egyptian border would disturb Shaima's chance to rest in peace, compelling her tormented soul to wander the Gazan badlands forever.

Gridlocked

Deprived

In my life, I have always tried to be a good person, to make the best of it, to find a little peace inside a war zone. I have tried to obtain a decent job, be a good family man, and give my children the best life possible. But life in Gaza is hard, very hard. The Strip of Death has so many unpredictable twists and turns. From war, violence, and missiles exploding on the beach, to the vast poverty and the subsequent hopelessness it generates. All these things make it difficult – impossible – to get ahead in life. When you are trying to survive in an open-air prison, a daily battle-ground, life is convoluted and chaotic. To begin with, we Palestinians are so poor that we must work as children. And the violence around us disturbs us so much that we are sleepless and cannot concentrate at school anyway. As such, we don't get to finish school. This in turn, reduces our chances of getting good jobs. Gridlocked, get it? A grid or system of interlocking blocks and barriers working together to disadvantage and disempower us. With so many walls and obstacles, we do not make the slightest progress in life whatsoever.

In Gaza, I never finished primary school at all. Why? I had to start working at the age of 12 to support my family. I clearly remember the day I started my first job. I felt so grown-up back then – getting up early each morning just like the other adult men who were working to earn money and help their families. At the time, I got a job working in a local metal shop. At first, I helped out however I could. I would sweep the floor, clear away rubbish, keep the place tidy, or run small errands for the store. The manager paid me a very small wage, which was just 5 shekels a day (US$1). I knew it was not a lot, but I felt good helping my family. As they say, "Every little bit helps." In those days, I would leave for work every morning and return back home in the evening feeling satisfied that I had earned a little money all by myself without having to rely on anyone else. I was just a naïve young boy back then trying to survive. I didn't think that my lack of schooling would hurt and disempower me later, by diminishing my chances of getting decent employment in the future.

As soon as I reached adulthood, I tried to find a better job. In 1999, three members of the Zanoon clan, my cousins Rafat, Farhood and Majed, decided to travel across the border into Israel to look for work. And I joined them. It was very easy to enter Israel back then because there was no fully blown war happening at the time. These days it is impossible for a Palestinian to enter Israel, especially after the launch of the 2014 Gaza War. Anyway, it took us a while to find employment in our neighbouring country. Eventually, however, all four of us got jobs working in a large metal shop together. The store manager was a man from Jerusalem named Wajde – who happened to be from Palestine. I felt happy and proud to be working alongside a fellow Palestinian. Wajde seemed to be very nice at first, guiding us at the store and telling us interesting things about Israel. But as I got to know him over time, I learned different. The work was hard – much harder than what I had been doing previously. For example, my cousins and I had to start work at 6am and keep working nonstop until 10pm. We also learned that the price of accommodation in Israel was so expensive that we couldn't even afford to live anywhere, not even after pooling all our money together! So every night after work we huddled together on the factory floor. It was very cold at night sleeping on the hard concrete surface. We had no mattresses, no blankets, and no pillows. We would just lie there all night – and shiver. As if that wasn't bad enough, the workshop was full of mosquitoes. Every night when we tried to sleep, we ended up being feasted on. Then, after a sleepless night of feeding hungry mosquitoes, we would wake up every morning to find ourselves covered from head to toe in hundreds of bites from these bloodthirsty little insects.

After working at the metal shop for several weeks, we hadn't received any pay. Well, one day we plucked up the courage to ask our manager to pay us our wages. We approached Wajde and asked: "Please, can we have our wages?"

"WHAT?!" he replied angrily.

"Can we please have our wages now?" we repeated.

"How dare you ask me for money! I don't owe any of you *anything*. You slept in *my* workshop and I *fed* you, and now you have the nerve to ask me for *money!*" he shouted angrily at us.

The four of us just stood there in shock.

"If any of you mention money to me again I will call the police and have you all thrown in jail!"

I couldn't believe it. We had worked so hard for a couple of months for this Palestinian man, and it was all for nothing! At that moment, Wajde's one greedy sting for money was more painful than if all the hungry blood-sucking mosquitoes in Israel were biting me at once!

Straight after this disappointing work experience, we all decided to leave Israel and return home to Gaza to our families. We crossed the border into Gaza and headed back home. It was good to be home again. I had missed everyone so much during my stay in Israel. But I was sad and guilty too. How embarrassing to return home empty-handed after working so hard in Israel all that time. After a few days, I started working in my old job again at the local metal shop. I had to start saving money from scratch. But I didn't get a chance to save any money at all. Not long after I started working there, the Al-Aqsa Intifada broke out (the second Palestinian uprising against Israeli occupation and a period of intense Israeli-Palestinian violence). It started in September 2000 and a blockade was imposed at the border. Many people lost their jobs as a result of this blockade because they couldn't cross the border to get to work. My goal to save money was ruined. My career in the metal workshop was short-lived. My opportunity to get ahead was blocked. I was unemployed. Gridlocked again, as usual.

Demented

A number of months had passed by after I returned home from Israel. I remember being at home with my family watching television. All of a sudden, we heard the sound of gunshots firing rapidly in the streets. I got up and went outside to see what was happening. I noticed the Hamas Terrorist Forces driving around in their black cars, their faces completely covered with black balaclavas. All of them were carrying large guns and repeatedly shooting up at the sky. It seemed like they were celebrating something really important. But what?

The Hamas continued firing their torrent of bullets madly into the sky nonstop for at least ten minutes. They were yelling loudly and whistling like crazy too. In the midst of this commotion, a Hamas party member rolled down the window of his black 4WD truck and started making public announcements through a set of large speakers loaded on the back of his vehicle. I watched him lift the microphone up to his mouth. But I never expected to hear such chilling words to pass his lips:

"Kill all Americans!

Kill all Israelis!

Kill all non-Muslims!"

What?! Why does this Hamas man and the rest of his terrorist group want to kill innocent people for? In Israel, America, and the world?

I had no idea what was happening. I just stood there and watched the Hamas' macabre revelry. After the Hamas spokesman finished making his global death threat he started throwing sweets at all the onlookers who had gathered in the streets. Huh? Everyone was so confused. Why was all this strange activity happening? What was the reason behind this disturbing festivity?

The Hamas continued to shower the crowd with sweets. The Hamas man's microphone voice sounded exhilarated with whatever was happening. He started shouting even more loudly and excitedly:

"*Kill all Israelis!*

Kill all Americans!

Kill all non-Muslims!

Kill all Israelis!

Kill all Americans!

Kill all non-Muslims!"

How could he be allowed to say such things? To advertise a killing spree in public? I felt sick to my stomach after seeing and hearing such terrible words come out of his dirty mouth. After that, I left the crowded streets and returned home. When I got there I turned on the television and switched over to a news channel to see if I could find out why the Hamas Terrorist Organization were celebrating so fiercely. And then, I saw it. "*OOOH NOOOOO!*" I cried in horror.

The news explained it all. No words could ever describe the terror I felt when I saw that historic and unforgettable news flash about the event that shook and shocked the world.

It was September 11, 2001. A terrorist group named Al Qaeda had hijacked two passenger planes and crashed them into two tall office buildings that were part of the World Trade Center in New York. As a result of this and other violent terrorist attacks that day, over three thousand people lost their lives. Three thousand *innocent* people – people on airplanes kidnapped by the terrorists, people who were working in buildings, and people who were just walking in the street. *"How could anyone celebrate such a treacherous deed?"* I thought. *"How can the Hamas be happy when families everywhere had just seen their loved ones die in a horrific way? How can the Hamas even imagine rejoicing such cruel and unnecessary deeds? What have those innocent people ever done to hurt Hamas and Al Qaeda? Nothing! They never did a thing wrong! Yet, that day all those people lost their lives because a stupid extremist group would rather instigate war, mass destruction and senseless killing than promote a world of peace!"* I will never, ever understand the rationale behind this dark and demented act on that fateful September day. Or, even how a political group could use Islam, or any religion for that matter, to justify violence. This terrorist attack sent shockwaves throughout the world that it had never seen before. Meanwhile, in Gaza, I watched the Hamas in horror as they celebrated their spectacle of shame. I sank deeper into despair thinking that the world had finally ended. Then – instantly and radically – Gaza felt like a very dangerous place to be. My heart skipped a beat and a cold current of fear shot down my spine.

Decided

Now I am 27 years old, but I feel as if I am 67 years old. The adversity of war doesn't just make you grow up emotionally, it ages you – fast. I have seen, heard and experienced too much terrorism, too many terrible things for one person to bear. All the while, we Gazans have only ever wanted a peaceful life and peace for our children so that they can build a good future for themselves and their families.

"Please stop the fighting. We don't want it. We want to live together in peace."

"Gaza needs a future for the children," we Palestinians would shout.

"God, please give Palestine back. Please bring peace to our land," people in our community cry. "May Muslims and Jews and others live in harmony – together we can build a better world." And: "A life without war, peace for our children, that's all we Palestinians want." This is what the people of Gaza want and talk about. This is what the graffiti boards in Palestine write about.

This is what our hearts genuinely desire. But peace is just a dream that has never happened. It is still not happening in the year 2014. Maybe it never, ever will happen. It is no wonder, then, that at home in Gaza, when I went to bed at night to sleep, I couldn't. All I could do was think about our pathetic plight. We had no freedom and we definitely had no peace. All the militant Hamas Government wanted to do was to fight and cause trouble with our neighbouring Israel. To this day, my Gazan friends are still screaming things out like: "Jews, Christians, Muslims – we're all human beings. The problem isn't with the people. It's a conflict between governments." But who is listening? Who wants to help us? No one, it seems. When people's ears are blocked, we are more gridlocked. No one wants to hear people screaming in hell.

More and more, I sensed a change happening inside me. I guess I had to change. I had to adapt in order to survive – to break free. The day of the drive-by shooting, the day that Israeli snipers shot my cousin in the street, the day Hamas extremists shot my friend and blasted my arm – such events changed my life forever after that. I realised that my family wasn't safe. My children weren't safe. And I, especially after a religious Hamas zealot promised to assassinate me, definitely wasn't safe in Gaza anymore. My experiences turned my deepest belief system upside down. After that, I didn't want to be a Muslim anymore. Islam is supposed to be a religion of peace but all the Hamas ever do is talk about fighting and killing everyone in the name of "Islam". At first, those of us who wanted to live in peace arranged and attended demonstrations to try and get the pro-Hamas Government to make life easier in our own country. But it simply didn't work. Things didn't get easier for us at all. Rather, things got harder for us. Life got worse, much worse. The power was cut, protesters were imprisoned, and innocent individuals were tortured or killed. Sometimes, people who campaigned calmly just 'disappeared' from our community, never to be heard of again. In many different ways, we were being barred, blocked and gridlocked by a corrupt and treacherous government.

After seeing the death of so many innocent people, the death of my friend and cousin, after being shot at in the street, and after seeing my family suffer and children starve, I decided to renounce Islam, and leave Gaza forever, and the atrocious hellhole it had become. I had seen too much violence here and I was extremely troubled as a result. I was desperate for peace. I was desperate to find a better way to help my family. After all, I was no good to anyone 'dead'. I was desperate to take a risk, to try something new, to do whatever it takes. All I did from then on was contemplate how I could leave this place. Day after day and night after night, I would sit just outside my front door and think about escaping Gaza. The big question was how?

How could I escape from Gaza? I was so gridlocked! After all, I was born in the Gaza Strip, Palestine. A document that proves my identity says I am a: "UN Palestine Refugee".

This means I have no nationality.

No country.

No rights.

I was born a refugee.

I lived my whole life a refugee.

I am a refugee.

I will die a refugee.

Every time a way out of Gaza appeared, so did some wall, barrier, or obstacle to block my escape. Gridlocked, gridlocked, gridlocked. For example, being a Palestinian makes it much harder for us to obtain visas to travel to *any* country. Believe me, I thought of many ways to leave Palestine in a simple, straightforward way. But I couldn't. I was stopped at every turn before I could even start. One idea I had was to secretly cross the border. But this is not practically possible. The Gaza border is closed. Its borders are blocked by high concrete walls and huge gates. On one side, the borders are watched and patrolled by the Egyptian army, who do not allow any Palestinians to enter their country. A more sinister eye watching the border of Gaza is the Hamas Terrorist Group. These Islamic radicals would shoot anyone attempting to flee Palestine. In fact, they shoot people for no reason at all.

In particular, I thought of leaving Palestine as a refugee the right way, the proper way, the bureaucratic way. But that did not work. I planned to visit a United Nations (UN) office for help. In Palestine, however, we don't have one! I tried applying for a visa to live in England three times. And three times they rejected me because I had no job, no house, no family, and no money there. I also travelled to Malaysia to apply for a visa there. The Malay immigration authorities told me it would take more than six years to process my application. Well, that option was no good to me either. Nedal, the young Hamas man who shot me, would make sure I was well and truly dead by then. In fact, it took me seven years to explore 'proper' ways to leave Gaza after I was shot, all the while living in fear that I could be murdered at any moment by Nedal. Clearly, since Gaza was such a strong fortress and more, I was so firmly gridlocked that I had to start thinking more desperately. In the end, I figured that my only chance to escape the deadly Gaza Strip was to do so deviously. I became so desperate that I started plotting ways to enter other countries *illegally*.

Departed

I had had enough.

I could not take the fighting anymore.

I could not live in fear of my life anymore.

I could not let my family suffer anymore.

I could not watch my children's faces grow sadder anymore. Waking up every day to the idea that a terrorist wants to shoot me and unable to provide properly for my family, I decided:

I can't go this way.

I can't go that way.

I don't have freedom.

I don't have peace.

I am not safe.

I don't want war.

I don't want someone to kill me.

I don't want to die.

Despite my deep love for my two sons and my family, it was too dangerous for me to stay.

I had to leave my two sons Jehad and Rayan behind, leave my mum, dad, brothers and sisters, my home, my family, and everything I knew. I had to leave Gaza forever.

After making my difficult decision, the day came when I would finally depart Gaza. And there was only one way out of here. I had saved some money, sold everything I owned, and borrowed as much money as I could from people I knew. I packed a small bag of personal belongings. A phone, laptop, ID cards, money, some clothes, and a few family photos. I was finally taking my first step to a new and better life.

It was the 3rd of May 2013 and a cold, crisp spring morning when I left my family, my home, and my old life in Gaza forever. I will never forget that sad but exciting day, starting a journey to find peace in another part of the world. This was the life I always wanted, dreamed about, longed for so much – to live in peace and have a good job. On an early May morning, in the company of my father, I arrived at the Palestinian-Egyptian border. At this time, people were forbidden to enter Egypt unless they were accompanied by a parent. It was about 5am and very cold. The high steel gates were due to open at 9am and people were already piling up to cross over. After going through the long process of waiting in the queue with my dad for several hours, I reached the point of crossing the border from Palestine into Egypt. My father turned to me for the last time and looked at me with tired brown eyes. The last thing he ever said to my face was: "Raed, look after yourself. May God be with you always." Tears streamed down his wrinkled cheeks, and for a moment he didn't look like the angry, abusive, pot-throwing dad I was so familiar with. "Look after my two boys and our family, Dad," I said to him, kissing his cheek. Then I walked through the Gaza Gate, feeling sad, excited, scared and brave all at the same time. It felt like I was crossing a magic doorway into a whole new world, knowing I could never return to the old one again. I would be killed if I did. I had just taken the first step of my long journey to peace. I was finally escaping deadly Gaza.

It was a long taxi ride from the Egyptian border to Cairo that day. Although I had undertaken this journey before, it seemed to take longer this time. My arm, the one that was shot, was hurting a lot and the pain didn't help. The further and further that I went from Gaza, the closer I got to my dream of a peaceful and better life. At last, seven hours later, I reached Egypt's capital – Cairo. It was very late at night when I arrived at the airport and I had to lie down and sleep. I found a cosy corner on the airport floor and curled up there to rest. I slept at the airport for the rest of the night. I drifted in and out of sleep for ages. My sleep was interspersed with terrible nightmares about guns and death, as well as happy dreams about freedom, working, making new friends, and living a carefree life. Eventually, I woke up. Knowing how rife theft was in Cairo, I carefully checked to see if I had all my personal belongings with me before heading off to the departure gate. Everything went smoothly at the airport and after a while it was time to board my flight. "This is it!" I thought. "I will finally get peace in my life and a chance to help my family!" With a mighty roar, my plane thundered across the tarmac and soared high into the dark, night sky. I am not sure what time it was but I know it was about a four-hour flight to Qatar, my transit stop on the way to Indonesia. It was daylight when we landed in

Qatar. The landscape looked tremendously beautiful when I looked outside my window. A clear and confident female airline voice came over on the loudspeaker: "It is time to disembark this plane and go to the transit lounge." So I waited in the transit lounge for my flight. My wait was going to be a long one, so I decided to take another nap before my next flight. I drifted into a deeper sleep than the one I had in Cairo. This time I had no nightmares, just nice dreams – working, playing and laughing with family. When I awoke, it was time to take the next step of my long and exhilarating journey.

Dark Jakartan Jungles (2013)

On the 5th of May 2013, I finally arrive in steamy, tropical Indonesia. It is just 48 hours after leaving Gaza. Once I arrive at the airport in Jakarta, I make a call to an Iraqi man whose number was passed down to me through a series of covert contacts. The person's name was Abo Tariq and he works in the 'people-smuggling' trade. This surreptitious business involves transporting people with no visas from Indonesia to Australia on fishing boats. I have always wanted to go to Australia – I have heard so much about it being a safe, free and happy place. And the only way I knew to get to Australia from Indonesia without a visa was by boat. Certainly, I have heard it is very dangerous. Many people drown. But I also know that in order to save my life, I must risk it. With no other options open to me, from England to Asia, I strongly believed that I had no other choice but to come to Australia by boat.

Once I arrive in Indonesia, I make the call to talk to a people smuggler.

"Hello. My name is Raed Zanoon. I am in Jakarta now and I want to go to Australia."

A low, slick voice answers: "I will send someone named Omar to meet you at the airport." And then I hear a 'click' as Tariq hangs up the phone. It doesn't take long for Omar, a thin and wiry Syrian man, to arrive and pick me up from the airport in a car. His eyebrows are so black and bushy that they look like a pair of big, fat leeches that have just glutted themselves with blood. I smirk uneasily to myself. To him, I guess I am 'fresh blood' in a way; I am a source of money and he will want lots of money from me as soon as possible.

We drive to an old run-down apartment building, where the next step of the journey is supposed to be arranged. With no chance to settle in at all, Tariq's assistant Omar gets straight down to business. "The journey costs US$6000," he says frostily. "You got it?" I tell Omar that I do not have enough money to pay for my journey. Then I show him what I *do* have: US$3600 cash, my laptop, and an iPad. Omar hesitates for a moment and thinks. "OK, then," says Omar. "To pay for your trip, I need *everything*." I part my lips to answer him but two scrawny hands are already scooping up the cash and snatching my laptop and iPad. I watch Omar's thin build slide out the door. Suddenly, fear overtakes me. I am totally alone. What can I do? I can't go anywhere now! I am alone in a strange country. I have no money, no food, no water, no contacts, and no way of communicating with my family or anyone else for that matter now that my computer is gone! As the night grows darker, so do my worries. What will happen to me? I have no idea. After a while, I hear a knock on the door and Omar steps inside. He has come to fetch me from the apartment to drive me to a big house. I learn from him that many people are already waiting at the house to take the same boat journey that I am about to take. When we arrive at the house, I notice many people from Iraq, Iran, Sri Lanka and other countries too. Omar gives me a message from Tariq that the people in the house will look after me. As soon as he tells me that, he leaves. I quickly learn that I am never meant to meet Tariq in person or ever see his face. I only have personal contact with Omar.

The next night, Abo Tariq calls the house to check if everyone is all right. When he calls, I anxiously tell him: "I cannot buy any food or water because you took all my money. You took everything from me. You left a message that other people in the house will give me food. But they haven't. You have left me with nothing!" But Tariq says nothing. He just hangs up the phone with a 'click'. When Tariq phones again a couple of days later, I say to him more desperately this time: "Look, I am sick. I need to leave this place." Once more, I hear another 'click' as he quickly hangs up the phone.

I feel very afraid to stay in this big house. Outside, I can hear the Indonesian police looking for people like me who come to Indonesia to travel to Australia by boat. If the police were to find us, they would arrest us and put us in an Indonesian immigration holding centre. These dangers, as well as the fact that I have no money, no contact with family or friends, and that I don't know anyone in Indonesia, force me to be a prisoner inside this house. I can't speak Indonesian, so I certainly can't arrange local help. Anxious thoughts and burning questions set my mind ablaze. *"What will happen to me? What will become of my family? Are these people smugglers just stealing my money with no intention of ever sending me to Australia? Will I make it out of here alive?"* When the bonfire in my brain burns down, my future looks bleak. The past was traumatic, the present is unclear, and the future is a completely crazy risk. I only have my faith in God to keep me going. So I pray. I plead with God to show mercy on me, to keep me safe, to protect my family, and to grant me my deepest wishes.

Four long days pass before I hear from Abo Tariq again. This time he delivers a message to the whole house. He says he is going to send someone to move five people from there soon, but he doesn't say how. I hope and pray that I am included amongst the first five. And I am. I don't know if I am chosen because God heard my prayer or if Tariq simply thought I was complaining too much. Nevertheless, the next morning a taxi drives up to the house and takes five of us away. Four Iraqi men and I climb into the waiting vehicle. We drive for five hours and reach what looks like a shopping centre. I look through the taxi window and I see about ten cars waiting for us. The vehicles look new, sleek, strong, and very, very black. They were black Jeeps with windows tinted so darkly that none of us could see inside the cars. All the cars look as if they belong to the Indonesian Mafia. We step out of the taxi after our long ride into the fresh air outside. It feels so good to stretch my legs at last but it is not for long. "Get into the car," a bossy Indonesian Mafia man orders.

Just like the cars, he too was very black – black jacket, black shirt, black trousers, black shoes and black sunglasses. I am sure he had a gun beneath that tailored black jacket. A thick gold necklace glinting in the sun illuminated his thick, thug-like neck. We all pile on to the soft leather seats of the Mafia cars – black, of course – and the vehicles surge ahead. Their engines snarl like hungry panthers hunting for food in the jungle. "I am so afraid," I think to myself as I have no idea what is going to happen to me and the others. "Are they just going to take us somewhere and shoot us? Only God knows," I sob.

This time we travel for ten or twelve hours. I keep thinking to myself: "Will this part of the journey ever end?" Sadly, no. We drive for another a day or so, stopping for brief toilet breaks in the lonely countryside. When we finally reach our intended destination, we are pushed out of the Jeep. I notice that we are standing outside a very large farmhouse. Nearby are some trailers or horse carts. "All of you, get out!" orders the Boss. After the Mafia men force us out of the cars, they load us up hurriedly on to the carts, pushing and prodding us on like cattle. Then they cover us with thick tarps to stop anyone from seeing us inside the carts. All I can hear around me are Mafia men shouting at us and shouting at each other. The Boss barks another order. And we are off again.

This time we drive for more than a day but no one really understands what is happening. We can't see anything through the tarp during the day, and at night it is pitch black outside. All I know is that I can hear other people travelling with us as part of a secret convoy in the Indonesian countryside. Our procession includes babies and young children. From the crying, coughing, and screams of pain I hear from time to time, some people seem very sick. And although I cannot see very well, I can tell that the car pulling our cart is driving very erratically, swerving from left to right all over the road. After about a day of travelling along crooked roads and hiding inside the cart, the vehicles pulling us finally stop. We climb out of our carts, slowly and stiffly. Every part of my body has cramps, aches, and pains from the cart ride. I look around and notice we are surrounded by a green leafy jungle and steep mountains. Not a house in sight and no people around for miles. The wilderness, the darkness, the remoteness – not to mention the rustling of jungle leaves nearby and strange, hissing noises coming out the thick green foliage (dangerous creatures and poisonous insects, no doubt) – make me feel too scared to breathe. My whole body trembles.

None of us knows what is happening. Everyone is so afraid. Many of the children start crying. At that moment, out of the thick, dark jungle, a car appears, driving up to where we are all standing. When it finally comes to a stop, a well-groomed woman steps out of the vehicle. She is wearing a leopard-print dress, a diamond necklace, and she looks like she has just stepped out of a beauty salon. In fact, I would say she looks like the wife of a wealthy Mafia man. Meanwhile, her dress helps her to look like a wild part of the dark jungle as if she rules it. Without a word, Jungle Queen motions to one of her assistants to hand out life jackets to us. At that moment, I breathe a long sigh of relief. The jackets are a sign that we will be sailing out of Indonesia soon. The whole time Jungle Queen does not talk to us at all. After she finishes overseeing the distribution of the jackets, she gets back to her car and leaves. The Mafia men push and shove everyone back into their carts once more. After the Boss gives his order, we are on the move again.

After a three-hour cart ride in the jungle, along rough and winding tracks, the Mafia men stop our hungry, thirsty, tired and scared group. "Get out!" the Boss shouts.

I look outside – it is very dark.

The voice of the Boss and other Mafia men shout loudly:

"Everybody with mobile phones, give them to me now!"

The people who have phones hand them in.

Many people in our group start crying – adults, children, and babies. We are so terrified at this point. We think the Mafia men are going to kill us on the spot, and then leave our bodies to rot somewhere on the damp rainforest floor. Despite our worst fears, however, we are not meant to die today. We are herded back on to the carts, the Boss gives the order, and we are off again. Another day's drive. This time the drivers speed ahead in such a hurry, I imagine a jungle predator leaping forward to pounce on its prey. The driver pulling my cart tears through the winding jungle path like a madman. I am so afraid I think I am going to have a heart attack and die right here and now under the tarp. After a while, our old carts and the slick, new Mafia cars that accompany us stop for the last time. We all climb out to commence what will be the last and hardest leg of our trek through the Indonesian wilderness. The Boss gets out of his car, lights up a cigarette, and then points with his index finger to an opening in the jungle. Then – just like that – without a word, the troupe of black Mafia men get back into their Jeeps and take off forever, leaving us truly alone in the dark Jakartan jungles. It was obvious what we had to do next. So we do it. We start walking in the direction the Boss pointed to, through the opening of the jungle, and right into the thick of it.

We walk for at least an hour through the trees – along slippery muddy paths, up and down steep, stony tracks in the hills. The mountain trail is tricky and treacherous. I notice that the children and old people tire very quickly. When I glance behind me, I see one woman carrying a baby in her arms whilst three more children tug at her dress. I offer to carry the baby for her for a while. At first, she is unsure. But then, she lets me, smiling with relief. Towards the end of the hot walk through the gloomy monsoon rainforest, everybody starts to feel really tired and stressed. "Are we ever going to reach the ocean?" I keep thinking to myself. I am so exhausted by now that the idea of reaching the sea seems distant and unattainable. None of us understand what is going on or what is meant to happen next.

Suddenly, in the direction of a dim light coming from the distance, I hear a voice. It is yelling at us. "Come here! Come here!" a man's voice shouts. We all turn towards the voice and start walking in that direction. "What now?" I wonder. I am feeling so weak, tired, and afraid that I am starting to lose hope. As we get closer to the voice, the dense canopy thins out to reveal an amazing view. Not hemmed in by leafy palms and jungle vines anymore, I can see bright daylight ahead. Maybe it is midday. I step into the open. The sun is shining and the sky is bright blue. An ocean sparkles before me. It looks like a brilliant blue sapphire. I can see down at the water's edge a number of small boats bobbing up and down in the waves. Breeze, beach and boats. A tropical dream comes true.

It takes just a few moments to walk down to the beach. I notice that the white sand is like talcum powder underneath my weary feet, it feels so soothing. I just stand there in the bright sun, on the soft sand, by the blue sea, soaking up this lovely, carefree moment fully. It is very peaceful here. All of a sudden, an Indonesian man holding a shiny rifle steps out of the bushes, breaking the trance: "Give me all your money," he demands. What?! We just look at each other, stunned. Our mouths gape open. *What money?! No one has any money! Everyone has taken everything from us! There is no more money or anything at all left to give!* The Gunman looks angry. Panic sets in. We are very scared that the man with the gun will kill us for not having any money. Some people start to cry. But somehow, our poverty doesn't sit well with him. Gunman just scowls at us, letting off an angry grunt as he walks away. Despite one last, desperate attempt to rob us in this country, to squeeze blood from stone, greedy Gunman seems to accept our excuse and just goes about his business. Phew! Left to die another day once more.

I am still hungry and thirsty, not having eaten for some time now. But at least the next hour is tranquil. We just wait on the beach, finally getting a good rest and a well-earned stretch from all the hard and uncomfortable travelling. After leaving us alone for a while, Gunman starts waving small groups of people over to the boats. We are assembled, five or six people at a time, next to the small motorboats at the shore. We leave the coast behind for Gunman to patrol, and head out into deeper water. The sea is calm. The breeze is fresh. The horizon looks silver, blue and green. Opal-ish omens of a better life perhaps.

The boat ride lasts a few short minutes before we reach a larger vessel that looks much like... like... a rundown fishing boat? My feelings are mixed. I am really happy that I am finally sailing to Australia to live a free and peaceful life. And I know it won't be long before I am there. But the vessel we are travelling in also sets alarms bells off in my brain. This fishing boat looks too old, too unseaworthy, and far too small to carry 150 people! A lump rises in my throat. My mind starts to race. "Are we really going to sail to Australia on *this*? If so, will we actually make it there alive? Will we actually make it *out of the bay*?" I wonder, worry, and pray for all of us to stay safe. When we climb out of the small motorboats on to the shabby-looking fishing boat, I look around the deck for a place to sit. I find a spot on the edge of the boat.

As if the boat wasn't scary enough, my worries worsen dramatically when I see a small Indonesian man standing at the wheel. I think he is the captain of the vessel. But the look of him terrifies me. He must only be about sixteen years of age. What does a *teenage boy* know about the sea and boats? Nevertheless, we are all finally here – 150 people on a boat. Men and women, people from different countries, people with different backgrounds, and people of all ages from babies to teens to the elderly. But we all shared a few important things in common. All of us were about to set sail on an unstable, overcrowded fishing boat. All of us were crammed together on the same open deck, exposed to the same wild elements. Indeed, all of us were about to take a life or death journey to Australia. I hear boat's engine rev up and the seawater gurgle. Then, we head out to open water.

Outback Days

The Landing

Long, lovely beaches.

Friendly people, plenty of work, lots of time to relax.

A free and happy lifestyle.

This is the Australia I have always heard about and dreamt about my whole life.

Then, on the 17th of May 2013, the large navy ship that has rescued us at sea finally reaches Australia. But I do not make it to the mainland near world-famous icons such as the Sydney Opera House or Queensland's tropical beaches. Instead, I arrive on a rocky and rugged little island called "Christmas". It is obvious that the ship is far too big to pull up alongside the small jetty that looks like it is made of matchsticks. We must anchor in the shallows of the bay further out. After the ship is safely secured, the navy crew transfers us, about eight people at a time, into smaller speedboats, which take us right up to the shore. I notice some women waiting for us on the beach. When I reach them, I realise why they are waiting there. They hand everyone who leaves the ship a bottle of water and a pair of sandals. Then, from the shoreline, a minibus transports us to what will become my home for the next few weeks. It is a place called *Christmas Island Immigration Detention Centre*. Whilst staying here, I am given a boat number: "LYB094". You see, everyone who comes to Australia by boat without a visa is put into mandatory detention. This enables people to undergo immigration, security, and health checks.

When our Christmas Island bus arrives at the detention centre, a security officer in a light-blue shirt waits for us to disembark. I learn that security staff who work here are employed by a company called Serco. After we all get off, the greeting Serco officer leads us to a room to give us a pillow, towel, shampoo, soap, toothbrush and toothpaste. With fresh supplies in hand, he takes us to our rooms where I am finally reunited with the long-lost comforts of home. Each room contains three single beds, an air conditioner, a fridge and a television. "It will be so nice to sleep in a bed again," I think to myself. I take a few minutes to settle into my room and then I have a nice long shower for the first time in ages. The warm water feels good running over my skin, soothing my whole body. It is good to be clean and relaxed again. After showering, I have dinner, coffee, and then it is time to sleep. It has been so long since I have slept in a real bed, so you know what? I really look forward to it! That night – my very first night in Australia – I fall into a deep sleep. I feel calm and happy in my heart that I have made it safely to Australia. I have finally reached my dream.

The next morning I wake up and eat breakfast, and then I wander around the compound outside. Although I am inside an immigration detention centre, I can't help noticing how tidy and clean everything looks. So different to all the rubbish, debris and chaos scattered outside homes and buildings in the streets of Gaza. A blue sky, tall trees, and quiet surroundings make me feel happy. I also notice many Serco staff strolling calmly around the compound. The officers are friendly and they never seem to get angry with anyone. The best thing about Serco is the way they smile all the time, always greeting us with Australia's most famous phrase: "G'day, mate!", which they speak in happy Aussie accents. What's more, it is such a relief to see guards in the compound strolling around and not carrying weapons. This is so unlike the dangerously armed and trigger-happy soldiers back in Gaza. It feels fantastic and strange, to be in a place where you don't have to feel afraid of being shot or killed at any moment.

Later that morning I visit International Health and Medical Services (IHMS) for the first time. The IHMS doctor at the Health Clinic takes blood samples, physically examines all the recent arrivals, and checks everyone's health to make sure we are all right. When it is my turn to take the medical exam, the doctor notices a long, thick scar running down my arm. "What happened?" he asks with concern. I tell him a Hamas terrorist shot me in my arm and about all my health problems after that. The doctor listens and makes notes of what I say in my file. Once the medical check is finished, I am offered an opportunity to speak with an IHMS psychologist. This is the *first* time I have ever spoken to a mental health professional. Not knowing what to expect, I feel a bit nervous, but the psychologist is friendly enough. She just wants to listen to me and hear my story. I feel as if I can trust her, so I share my experiences and tell her all about life in Gaza. I tell her about my family, my wife, my two sons, and about the constant war and terrorism in my homeland. I find that talking about my painful experiences is a healing process. My soul feels lighter and brighter after that. When I finish speaking with the psychologist I am returned to the compound. A while later, I start to feel sick. My arm starts hurting and throbbing badly again. I try to rest and forget about the pain for a while, but I can't. As I lie on the bed in my room trying to sleep, I start worrying about my sons and my family back home. I wonder what my family is thinking about. *What are they doing? Are they all right? Do they need help?* More importantly, no one back home knows where I am or even if I am dead or alive.

On my second night in Australia, I have a terrible nightmare. I dream that a man on a horse is galloping through a dark forest towards me. Just as he is about to reach me, he raises his silver sword to strike me dead. The gleam of his sword against the dark background blinds my eyes. Oh, my head! I am in so much pain! At that very moment, I wake up in a sweat, screaming badly. I leap out of bed, open the door, and rush out of my room. I am not sure but I think the swordsman in my dream is still chasing me, pushing me out of my room with his terrible presence, determined to kill me. Am I asleep or awake? Is this a dream or reality?

It is not clear at all what is happening. I start yelling and screaming at the top of my voice outside. I'm not exactly sure, but I think people in the compound gather around my room to stare at me as if I have gone crazy. Maybe I am partly conscious because I hear a voice saying to me as I stand there shaking: "Raed, Raed, wake up." In a dreamlike state – not fully asleep, not fully awake – I somehow sense I am being taken to the health clinic. An IHMS doctor presses a cold damp cloth on my brow to cool me down. "Dark – s-word – k-k-kill me," I stutter as I try to tell the doctor about my nightmare. The doctor encourages me to relax, then gives me some pills to help me sleep. But I can't go back to sleep at all. That nightmare was so bad that I just can't go through it again. Bad thoughts start to take over my mind. Maybe there is no way to escape this terrible danger. Maybe I am better off dead. I start searching the compound for a good place to jump. A Serco officer notices my desperate behaviour so he takes me to the clinic again. An IHMS psychologist talks to me and tells Serco staff to watch me overnight. From then on, a male security officer observes me constantly. He takes me back to the compound, places a chair at the foot of my bed, and quietly sits there. I look at him and start to cry. Eventually, however, I fall asleep because I start to feel safe and comfortable. I think it was really nice of the psychologist to arrange a 'guardian angel' to watch over me that night.

The next morning the sun shines brightly and the day looks cheerful. The menacing mood of my scary dream has gone. After showering and eating breakfast, I see the same IHMS psychologist again. This time I tell her more about Gaza – the day I was shot in the arm, the day my best friend died, and other sad things. I am so touched by the way health staff seem care for me that when I return to the compound, I become lost in my feelings and my mind is deep in thought. A Serco officer seems to notice this so he pulls my attention back into the present: "Hey, Raed, you want to play a game?" he calls out. So I play ping-pong for a while, as he tells stupid jokes with his friendly Australian accent. I notice he was trying hard to make me happy, which was very kind. I look around and notice other refugees playing games with Serco too – cards, snooker, backgammon and football. Most of the people in the compound are just relaxing – sitting, chatting and drinking coffee. My arm starts to throb again, which makes me feel sick once more. I decide to go to my room, lie down, and go to sleep. But I can't. My mind recalls the terrible day my cousin was shot by a sniper. Then I see the faces of my children, my parents, and friends. I miss my family so much. Eventually, I fall asleep. And then, when I return to the dark world of dreams, an angry Hamas terrorist wielding an AK-47 machine gun appears. He is chasing me down a dark path, trying to kill me. I am running as fast as I can but he is gaining ground. He lifts up his rifle and it is aiming directly at my heart. I must have been shouting and screaming badly in my sleep that time because a Serco guard opens the door of my room to settle me. "Everything is all right, Raed. You are safe now. Please, try to sleep," he reassures me. He repeats his comforting words a few times and his soothing voice helps me to relax a little. I close my eyes and sleep until morning.

A couple of weeks later, my buzzing, confusing introduction to Australia blows over. All the new information starts to settle in my mind and my present reality sinks in. I learn from my own IHMS Health Records that I was much worse in detention than what I thought. Apparently, I was plagued by disturbing night-mares, psychosis, and suicidal behaviour that required me to take strong medication. I had to be supervised continually because I was at such a high risk of hurting or killing myself. To give you a glimpse inside the mental world of a refugee, here are just some health problems I had and the type of care I desperately needed from IHMS:

27/5/2013 – "Torture & Trauma" (Mental Health Nurse).

4/6/2013 – "Anxiety, panic symptoms, nightmares, and ruminative suicidal ideation" (Mental Health Nurse).

4/6/2013 – "Anxiety regarding reoccurring dream of a 'white horse' and being killed", "withdrawn", "often stays in his room" (Mental Health Nurse).

4/6/2013 – "Significant Torture and Trauma. Suicidal ideation. PLAN: See Psychiatrist. Supervise for suicide. Sleep medication" (Medical Doctor).

4/6/2013 – "Ongoing negative rumination all day and night. Preoccupied with thoughts of death. Tearfulness. Sleep problems. Nightmares. Panic and anxiety. Choking. Unable to Breathe. Thoughts of taking his life by jumping. 'Where can I jump from?' Looking for places to jump" (Mental Health Nurse).

6/6/2013 – "Placed on High Psychological Support Program (constant suicide watch). Suicidal thoughts and plans" (Psychologist).

6/6/2013 – "Woke in a very startled state at 3am. Not in his bed but on the concrete. Shouting and screaming in his sleep. Vivid nightmares of being hit with a machete and dragged behind a horse. Placed on constant suicide watch" (Mental Health Nurse).

6/6/2013 – "Sleep terror" (Medical Doctor).

6/6/2013 – "No control over his suicidal thoughts. PLAN: Remain on constant suicide watch" (Mental Health Nurse).

7/6/2013 – "Constant suicide watch. Torture and Trauma. Nightmares, panic, fear of death" (Psychologist).

7/6/2013 – "Fearful and withdrawn. Difficulty breathing as if 'someone is grabbing my throat'. Haunted by nightmares. Acute distress. Crying, wailing, lying on bed in a foetal position, unable to talk. Suicidal feelings. Place on Constant Suicide Watch" (Mental Health Nurse).

9/6/2013 – "Awoke hysterically. Feels possessed. Someone is moving his lips and controlling his mouth" (Mental Health Nurse).

9/6/2013 – "Suicidal thoughts. Severe Post-Traumatic Stress Disorder with dissociative episodes and prominent re-experiencing of trauma" (Psychiatrist).

9/6/2013 – "Nightmares. Disturbed Sleep. Depression. Post Traumatic Stress. Anxiety. Panic Attacks" (IHMS Health Records).

9/6/2013 – "Severe Post Traumatic Stress Disorder. Suicidal ideation" (Medical Doctor).

21/7/2013 – "Severe Post Traumatic Stress Disorder, Depression and Anxiety. Extensive input from Mental Health Team, Psychologist and Psychiatrist in detention. Charted Seroquel 25mg. Requires ongoing input" (Health Discharge Assessment for a Person leaving Immigration Detention).

As you can see, my life in Gaza was so bad and the nightmares were so bad, that I badly needed medical help. I guess the brutality of war shows that you can take a person out of war, but maybe you can't take war out of the person. That's when I started wondering: "Will I ever escape Gaza? Can I truly be free and live my future in peace?"

The Interview

I am nervous, so nervous that my hands are shaking. During my early weeks on Christmas Island, I am informed that someone from the Immigration Department wants to interview me. As such, I am taken to an interview room with a security camera. An immigration officer is waiting there for me in front of his computer. I pull a chair from under the desk and sit opposite him. The atmosphere is thick and tense.

"Why did you come to Australia?" the immigration officer wearing a blue uniform with a "DIAC" logo on his T-shirt asks me.

"In my country, there is no peace at all. There is war there and when I lived there, I was shot by a terrorist," I reply.

I roll up the sleeve of my shirt and show him my arm.

"The terrorist who shot me did this. He also killed my best friend," I continue, giving the officer my friend's name and the name of the terrorist too.

"What would happen if we returned you back to your own country?" the man asks.

"Every day my country is at war. If I am sent back there, I will be tortured in jail and killed," I reply truthfully. "The terrorist who shot me will shoot me dead next time he sees me. I would rather die here in peace than return to Gaza to die in terror there."

"Have you ever heard of a place called Nauru?" the man asks.

"If this place has peace, freedom and no bombs, then send me there. But I won't stop loving Australia," I say.

"Do you have any identification with you such as a passport, birth certificate, or driver's licence?" he asks.

"No... I threw them all into the sea when I was on the ship," I reply.

The immigration man stops typing for a moment and stares at me with a puzzled look on his face. "Why did you do that for?" he asks.

"I don't believe my passport and identification card will help me," I answer sadly. "Because I am a refugee from the Gaza Strip in Palestine," I explain.

I completely open up at the Immigration Interview and tell the man in the blue uniform everything about myself from the time that I am born. I tell him where I used to live, where I worked, the names of my family – everything.

The immigration man presses me about Nauru again.

"Yes, I would go there," I reply, "even though other people in the compound worry a lot about this place."

"Don't you have any form of identification at all?" he pushes.

"No! I told you, I have nothing!"

"Can you ask your family to send it here?" the man asks.

"OK, I will ask them," I reply uneasily, unsure if this will help my case or not.

The Immigration Officer gives me the postal address of the compound so I can ask my family to send me the necessary documents.

A few days pass and I am transferred from Christmas Island to another compound. This time I travel to *Curtin Immigration Detention Centre*. It is located on the Australian mainland at the top of Western Australia. It looks beautiful here – open and free. The staff and clients look happy and relaxed too. But I am nervous, so nervous my hands shake. This time, it's not because of an Immigration Interview. This time, it's because of all the deadly animals! Upon arrival, I am "advised on the presence of mosquitoes and snakes… Any snake sightings to inform Serco and not to touch it" (IHMS Health Record 6/7/2013). Adding to my lesson about poisonous reptiles, I also attend an information session about Australian law. When it finishes, I hear a familiar voice. I look around and recognise the immigration officer who interviewed me on Christmas Island.

"Raed? Can you please come with me?"

I am nervous again, so nervous that not only do my hands shake, this time my whole arm starts to twitch as well. We sit down together in an interview room and I notice the immigration officer is holding a report about me in his hand. He tells me about the law in this country and he also explains that Australians are good people. My arm twitches again.

"Maybe you will leave this detention centre soon. I want you to be ready. You could leave here anytime," he says.

I wonder what he means. Am I going to another detention centre? Or I am going out into the community? To live the free life that I have always dreamed about? I feel excited. Now I can't stop shaking or twitching at all. That evening, a Serco officer pushes a thin strip of paper under the door of my room. It reads:

Be ready in the morning because you'll be moving out.

I knew exactly what this meant. It was the best news I had heard in ages. I was finally going to live in the community, in a free and fair and friendly land called Australia. At long last, I would no longer live in fear of losing my life. No more bombs, no more attacks, no more guns. I try so hard to sleep that night, but I must admit, it is impossible.

Crossings

Red Cross

I am transferred to the hottest and highest capital city in Australia – Darwin. I clearly recall the moment that I stepped outside Darwin International Airport. The air was so hot and humid that I thought I would faint. Two women approached me. "Are you Raed?" one asked.

"Yes," I said, so she gestured to shake my hand.

"Welcome to Darwin! My name is Sally and I am your new caseworker from the Red Cross. This is Susie; she works with me. We are here to help you," Sally explained. How warm, friendly and sincere they seemed – just the way I imagined Australians to be. As we drove through Darwin, I couldn't tear my eyes away from the lovely, peaceful surroundings. Everything around me was so lush and green. The streets were lined with gum trees, palm trees, and tropical plants. It seemed like heaven to me. It was so unlike Gaza, a place full of stones, bricks, rubble, litter and the curse of ongoing war.

The people at the Darwin Red Cross helped me in many ways. First, they found me accommodation at a beautiful tropical elevated house in a suburb called Wanguri. The Red Cross also gave me some money "to help me get started," as Sally put it. After showing me my new home, Sally and Susie took me shopping. "This is the Casuarina Shopping Centre," Sally explained. There, my Red Cross caseworker bought me a SIM card and a mobile phone. I was so excited because my personal mobile phone was taken from me in Indonesia. Now, I could contact my family. We bought some food at the supermarket too and the range of goods there was wide – unlike anything back at home.

During the six weeks I lived in Wanguri, however, I became sicker due to the pain in my arm. Sally arranged for a doctor to examine me. "Mr Zanoon, you need an operation to fix the damage in your upper arm. But you need to be placed on a waiting list," the doctor explained. I felt overjoyed because somebody acknowledged that my arm still had a problem, and that the pain was not just a result of my imagination. To ease my pain in the meantime, the doctor wrote me a prescription for "tramadol". I thanked the doctor for her help. I also thanked Sally as she dropped me home. Here I was, in this wonderful country, in this big beautiful house, receiving the needed medical care. But I felt sad, something was wrong. It was not long before I realised that I didn't have anyone to share my new life with. My mind flooded with thoughts of my family back home and then I started missing them terribly. It might sound strange but I was happy and grateful, but really sad and lonely too.

After my short stay at the tropical house had expired, I had to find another place to live. I found a single room near the city centre with no furniture. I slept on the floor on top of my clothes. As I was not allowed to do paid work on the visa the Immigration

Department granted me, I couldn't earn any money to buy furniture. Worse, all day, every day, with no money to spend on activities, I found myself with nothing to do but just sit in my room, dwell on my past, and think about my family back home. I decided to contact Sally to tell her about this. All I can say is that I am so grateful to have the Red Cross support me. Although I couldn't do paid work, Sally suggested voluntary work. I liked this idea so we looked around for something appropriate. I got a work placement at the Red Cross clothes store in the Darwin city centre. I love this kind of work and everyone was so kind and helpful towards me. I really enjoyed working there.

On busy days, the work at the Red Cross Shop made me feel very tired. As such, sometimes I had to have long naps at home. That's when the nightmares returned. The terrorist, the one who shot me and killed my friend, was chasing me inside my head again. "I am going to kill you, Raed!" he kept threatening. I was half-asleep and not thinking straight at all when I grabbed a bottle of tramadol next to my bed, opened it, and poured all the pills into the palm of my hand. I vaguely recall raising my hand to my mouth slowly and swallowing all the tablets. I felt so numb inside. I started shouting and screaming at nothing, and then I think I collapsed on the floor of my room. The next thing I remember was listening to the voices of paramedics. Within minutes, I was in an ambulance on the way to the Accident and Emergency Department of the Royal Darwin Hospital. The doctors pumped the tablets from my stomach. After this, I was taken to a hospital ward where I believe I stayed for about four days. During this time, a new Red Cross worker named Shane came to visit me. He pulled up a chair and we chatted for a while. When I was well enough to be discharged, Shane came and drove me home from the hospital. I can never thank the Red Cross enough for all their help during my early Darwin days. According to my medical records from the Casuarina Family Practice, I was very unwell back then:

"Psychotic. Admitted to Cowdy ward for PTSD/Psychotic Episode"
(20/12/2013).

At times when I am alone at night, I wonder what will become of me. I was terrorised and traumatised in Gaza. I cannot stop the nightmares in Australia. "Will I ever find the happiness and peace I am looking for?" I keep asking myself over and over.

Christian Cross

As soon I felt well enough to work at the Red Cross again, I did. This time, I met a new volunteer named Gary Miller. Gary told me about a church he attended called the Darwin Baptist Church and about Christian life, which I found fascinating. "Come with me to church on Sunday," said Gary.

"Sure, that would be really nice," I replied. When Sunday came Gary picked me up and drove me there. I listened to all the messages and hymns attentively. At this church, nobody talked about war, fighting or killing people. I could feel love and positive energy from everyone. It was so peaceful there.

Everyone asked for my mobile number so I gave it to them. Although I was missing my biological family in Gaza, I now felt as if I had a new spiritual family in Darwin. I attended Bible classes and learned about Jesus Christ. Sometimes, I prepared food from my homeland for everyone to taste. Everyone loved the Palestinian dishes that I cooked. We tried to make it a regular event. One day I received a copy of the Holy Bible in Arabic. I was so happy to receive this gift. Later, my new friend Curt took me fishing for the first time in my life. The very first time I casted out my line I caught four fish. I was so pleased and excited. Every day, my new Christian friends called me and asked me to join in some activity. I always agreed as long as I wasn't a bother to them. Eventually, I became baptised and became a Christian.

Several months of helping the Red Cross and attending church passed. At that time, I finally received news about my arm surgery. When the day of my operation finally arrived and I went into hospital, I was happy and scared. I knew that in a matter of hours the metal plate in my arm causing all the pain would be removed. But I also worried if the pain and problems would continue. After several hours of surgery, in the recovery ward, the first thing I saw when I opened my eyes were two friends from church. "Hey Raed… welcome back!" said Adam. "How do you feel?" asked Alistair. In fact, a number of people visited me, leaving me with food, flowers and gifts. When I returned home from hospital, Gary and other friends from church came to visit me. We spoke about God and how blessed I was. I couldn't wait for Sunday to come around so I could go to church and thank God myself. When Sunday arrived, I went to church, knelt down, and prayed very hard that day.

Cultural Crossfire

In Darwin, the *Northern Territory News* did something bold and kind. They published a really positive news article about refugees. Actually, it was a story about me. On the 29th of April 2014, journalist Courtney Todd wrote about my "gratitude for a life free of fear":

Palestinian refugee Raed Zanoon wants to say thank you to Australia after receiving surgery to fix an eight-year-old bullet wound. He was born and raised in a refugee camp in Gaza City and for most of his life he has lived surrounded by death and fighting. "A Muslim terrorist shot me in the arm, the bullet went through my arm and killed my friend."

The bullet broke his humerus in several places, requiring a metal plate to hold the bone together. But his arm remained weak and painful, and whenever it ached he had nightmares about the man who shot him. For seven years, he lived with the pain and the fear until he couldn't take it anymore.

The Royal Darwin Hospital... removed the metal plate and fixed visible damage. "Thank you" to [the] Red Cross and the doctors. "I'm sorry I came by boat but if I had peace, safety and freedom in my country I wouldn't have come."

I guess it was a nice story about a person who came to Australia to escape death and terrorists. However, soon after my news story was published, I received 13 posts on the Internet about the story from people all over Australia. Their comments really surprised me:

A person called *The average Australian of Darwin city* wrote: "We still have waiting lists out the doors for our own countrymen and women to go under the knife. Great story but it doesn't make the many of us actual citizens rest easy at night knowing they are getting medical attention before we are! *(Posted at 2:23pm, April 29, 2014)*

Al mompo of cairns wrote: "No sympathy for people who refuse to follow our rules. Real refugees don't travel 5000km by plane with a valid visa to enter Indonesia/Malaysia then [pay] another $10–20,000 to board a boat for Australia without [a] valid visa. Why not just pay $2400 for a ticket to Sydney after having applied for a tourist visa. What do they have to hide?" *(Posted at 2:31pm, April 29, 2014)*

Gerty Mcfarlane of Darwin wrote: "They pay tens of thousands of dollars and leave their whole family behind, talk about self-centred; he's never been an honest refugee. Mr Zanoon would not know the word honest if it hit him [in] the face." *(Posted at 9:13pm, June 6, 2014)*

It made me incredibly sad that people in Australia were so upset about me receiving surgery on my arm. I did not mean to offend anyone. Maybe some people don't understand what is really going on in other parts of the world. Or how hard it is to get out of Gaza. Why didn't I apply for a visa and just fly to Australia? Well, because the immigration department would have rejected any visa application from me to visit here, in case I was going to apply to stay on the grounds that Palestine is at war. Why didn't I bring my whole family to Australia with me? Well, because it took me a few years to save up several thousand American dollars just to pay the people smugglers for one boat ticket. It would take a century to save a million dollars to bring my whole family by boat. Also, I was the one that a Muslim terrorist wanted to kill, not my family.

So what if people hate refugees? What's the big deal? I guess the problem is that people go on fighting with each other. Wars are fought, people are tortured, individuals are killed and discrimination grows stronger. Hate breeds hate. Over time, hostile attitudes from people like the ones I describe here can develop a dark life force of their own, triggering wars just like the ones that are happening now in Gaza and in other countries around the world.

Gaza Falling

It is a cool Darwin evening and another red sun sinks down into the Arafura Sea. High above the palm trees in my garden, black cockatoos call loudly to each other as they fly across the sky. During the dry season, Darwin sunsets are so serene. I recline back into my comfortable bed, the one that Julie-Anne bought for me, and turn on the TV to watch the news. A story about Palestine is on the air. On the 12th of June 2014 three Israeli teenagers were kidnapped in Gush Etzion in West Palestine. Eighteen days later their bodies were found dumped in an open field near Hebron. Although the Hamas Terrorist Group denied this gruesome triple murder, I sincerely believe they were behind it.

A few days later, a 15-year-old Palestinian youth was kidnapped by Israeli locals. Gasoline was poured all over his body and down into his intestines through his mouth. Then they set him alight. The poor boy was burnt alive as retaliation for the Israeli teenage killings. The tension in Gaza between the Israeli Government and the Hamas Terrorist Organization grew so quickly that Israel began placing army forces along the Gazan border. Of course, when I heard this news I instantly became worried about my family there. With army forces strengthening, I knew there would be big trouble soon. I guess I was right because a few days later bombs started raining down from the sky on to the innocent residents of Palestine. As soon as I heard the grave news, I just sat in my room and cried. "Please, God, protect my family and all the people in Gaza. Keep everyone safe," I prayed as hard as I could.

Since the start of the Gaza War in July 2014, the worst one to date, I have not slept properly at all. I have spent practically every waking moment sitting in front of the TV watching the news and just hoping and praying that I wouldn't see anyone I knew reported dead. Over the course of just a few weeks, the warfare intensified so badly that about 2000 innocent Palestinians, many of whom were women and children, were killed. The Israeli forces even bombed schools and UN shelters where people sought refuge. *Nowhere is safe in Gaza.* I can't sleep at all these days because I fear for my family's safety. The only thing I think about now is my family and my children. All this time, whilst the fierce Israeli assault on Gaza has been killing innocent people and bombing the homes of harmless civilians above ground, the Hamas has been hiding and surviving in the underground tunnels.

A few nights ago, I turned on my computer and contacted my family on Skype:

"Hello, Raed," my father's voice answered.

"Hello, Dad. Dad – I am so worried about you all!"

"Yes, son, the situation is very bad here."

"I know, I have been watching TV," I replied.

"We have no water, no food, and the electricity supply only lasts about an hour a day."

"Can't you all get into Egypt where you will be safe?"

"No, Raed. All the crossings are closed."

After hearing this from my father, tears started falling from my eyes. I know my family is in danger and can be killed at anytime. I was so afraid for them all that I couldn't stop crying.

"Dad? I need to speak with Jehad and Rayan, please," I sobbed.

My father wiped away his tears away and called to my sons. First, I speak with Jehad.

"Hi, Jehad. How are you?" As soon as he heard my voice, he started to cry. "I am scared, Baba."

"I know you are, son, please be strong."

"Baba, I am very scared, I need you with me."

As fast as a sure and straight arrow, my son's words pierced my heart. My eyes filled up with water. Then I saw my mum smiling and waving at me through the camera. I waved back at her. I knew that my family was getting ready to die. As devote Muslims, they look forward to Heaven. That is a special place where there will be no more helicopters, gunfire, explosions, or suffering.

Since August 2014, the situation in Gaza has worsened. The ground forces have invaded Rafah. My father explained that nearby explosions have destroyed my family's house and that all my relatives have left their homes because it is not safe there anymore. Some nights the people of Gaza sleep in schools, and sometimes no one knows where to sleep. This makes me more afraid because a few days ago the news reported that Israel started bombing schools. I remember what it was like when ground troops entered Rafah during the 2009 Gaza War, so I know just how dangerous the situation can get. It breaks my heart that everyone I love must go through yet another terrible war just because of an evil action triggered by terrorists. It seems so long ago since I have slept. In fact, I cannot sleep at all – not even after taking pills. All I do is worry about my family.

The other night, after two hours of poor and restless sleep, I switched on the TV to hear the latest news bulletin: "BREAKING NEWS – a 72-hour ceasefire will come into effect tomorrow at 8am local time." I felt so relieved knowing everyone in Gaza would be safe even though it would be only for a very short time. But just two hours in, the ceasefire was broken by rocket fire from both sides. Heavy bomb raids started again so I tried to call my father. This time his mobile was turned off. So I tried to ring the rest of my family who have phones. Their phones were cut off too. I feared the worst. I have been trying to Skype my family for several nerve-racking days now, but there has been no connection. I have not heard anything from anyone for too long.

All I do is watch television. The latest news update reports that the Israeli army has been aggressively bombing and demolishing the smuggling tunnels in Gaza. My heart races. These underground tunnels are situated only a minute away from my family's home. Feelings of sadness overwhelm me as I watch images of dead and injured children on TV. I have been praying really hard to God not to see my own children dead on the news. So much destruction in Gaza, with thousands of people killed, wounded and displaced. Many innocent civilians are left with nothing at all because of a war between two governments: Hamas and Israel. Although my worst thoughts and feelings overwhelm me, the latest tragedy in Gaza still stirs to life my survival instinct, that part of me that war and terrorism have not been able to destroy. My fighting spirit suddenly screams out:

"Save the innocent people of Gaza!
Free Palestine!"

As the Gaza War blazes in Palestine, it also burns inside me. The deadly Gaza Strip is part of me now. I have risked my life staying in Gaza to live with the war. I have protested peacefully with people in Gaza to stop the war. I have also risked my life escaping Gaza – to flee its deadly war. I don't want to die in front of my children just because a terrorist wants to shoot me in the heart. So I travelled from one side of the world to the other in the most treacherous and humiliating way possible... as a boat person. But for what? To find out that I may never escape Gaza and its terror?

The past haunts me, the present challenges me, and my future is unclear. That is why I want to share this story with you. Maybe if other people know what is happening in Gaza, then they will be wiser about the wider world: who terrorists are, what life is like in their midst, and all the people they want to kill. Maybe my story can encourage people who live in freedom not to judge and hate refugees so quickly. I would rather have you as my friend, than my critic or my enemy. I would rather cook my mum's tastiest Palestinian dishes for you, than to fight with you and make life on both sides miserable. I prefer that we find ways to cast aside any distrust or misunderstanding that threaten to tear apart our hearts, our world, and the future of our children. The more friends we make, the less enemies we will have. As such, the more chance everyone all over the world will have to escape and erode wars like those in Gaza. I truly believe that all people would choose peace over war and that deep down, we're all passionate peace-seekers. No matter who we are or where we come from, I think that every struggling heart has a deep desire to set its inner peace dove free.

References

Anonymous. "Australian Humour. It's different and baked by a Bigger Sun."

http://www.australianinspiration.com.au/Quotes/Australiana/Humour.aspx (viewed 25/07/2014)

Coleridge, Samuel Taylor (1772–1834) *The Rime of the Ancient Mariner.*

http://www.poets.org/poetsorg/poem/rime-ancient-mariner (viewed 25/07/2014)

Jacob, Anna. "The wings of hope carry us, soaring high above the driving winds of life."

http://izquotes.com/quote/296084 (viewed 25/07/2014)

Todd, Courtney (2014) "Refugee's gratitude for a life free of fear." *Northern Territory News*, 29/04/2014, page 2

Todd, Courtney (2014) "Palestinian refugee Raed Zanoon thanks Australia after receiving surgery."

http://www.ntnews.com.au/news/northern-territory/palestinian-refugee-raed-zanoon-thanks-australia-after-receiving-surgery/comments-fnk0b1zt-1226899254448 (viewed 08/08/2014)

"Yea, thou I walk through the valley of the shadow of death... of mine enemies," *Bible*, American Standard Version (1901) Jewish Publication Society.

http://www.kingjamesbibleonline.org/psalms-23-parallel-kjv-asv/ (viewed 25/07/2014)

Book Category Themes
Autobiography

Converting from Muslim to Christian
Current Affairs
Overcoming Adversity
Asylum Seekers/Refugees
Terrorism

BOOKS

O is a symbol of the world, of oneness and unity; this eye represents knowledge and insight. We publish titles on general spirituality and living a spiritual life. We aim to inform and help you on your own journey in this life.

Visit our website: http://www.o-books.com

Find us on Facebook:
https://www.facebook.com/OBooks

Follow us on Twitter: @obooks